A JUDITH MARKHAM BOOK

Virginia Stem Owens

A FEAST
OF FAMILIES

Zondervan Publishing House
a Division of The Zondervan Corporation
Grand Rapids, Michigan

A FEAST OF FAMILIES

Library of Congress Cataloging in Publication Data
Owens, Virginia Stem.
A feast of families.
1. Family. 2. Life.
3. Christian life—1960-
4. Owens, Virginia Stem. I. Title.
HQ518.O9   1983
306.8'5   82-21773
ISBN 0-310-45850-1

The portion of this work entitled Prologue
was first published as
"One Wish for Your Children"
in *Today's Christian Woman,* Winter 1982-83,
© 1982 by Fleming H. Revell Company, Old Tappan, New Jersey.

Designed and edited by Judith E. Markham

Printed in the United States of America

83 84 85 86 87 88 — 10 9 8 7 6 5 4 3 2 1

For
Jennie Dobbs,
Mae and Grady Ward Adams,
and
Mayflower Lively

Contents

feast / fēst [ME *feste* festival, holiday, feast] something partaken of or shared in with delight; a religious festival of rejoicing.

Webster's Third New International Dictionary

Prologue

What do you want for your children?" a friend asked me last week. "If you could give them, like the fairy tale godmother, some good gift, what would it be?"

"I'm not going to say happiness, if that's what you're expecting," I told her. "That's too deceptive. It might not be what's good for them." I used the classic maternal line without apology.

"All right then. What?"

The fairy godmother's job, I discovered, is harder than one might suppose. To put into one sensibly wishable sentence what you hope for your child, to pack into a few syntactically strung words a wish that will take into account at once all the lurking hazards of life while leaving enough growing room, like a coat bought to last more than one season, for expansion in unpredictable directions. Finally I cleared my fairy godmother throat and said tentatively, "I want them to fulfill their destinies."

My friend gave me a sidelong look as though I had cheated at the game and immediately began pushing me into a more definitive corner. Did I mean marriage?

I shrugged.

A religious . . . (now she seemed at a loss for words) a religious aspect?

Of course. Destiny is definitely a religious term for me.

Would any religion do? Would I be satisfied with a good Buddhist? A Mormon? A Moslem? Any kind of recognition of a spiritual dimension to life? Or would I insist on Christianity?

Yes. Definitely Christianity.

She paused a moment, a little surprised at my quick response to her last question. Then she said, "I agree. I think it's important to be faithful to your heritage. I was brought up a Presbyterian, and I believe it is a valuable way of approaching God. I would want to see my children continue in that tradition. Anything else would seem sort of phony to me. Faddish. Of course, if I'd been raised a Buddhist, I'd probably feel the same way about Buddhism."

I sat there struggling internally with this. That wasn't what I meant at all. For one thing I had *not* been brought up a Presbyterian. I had confronted the fact years ago that my reasons for rejecting my own family's rich denominational heritage were based largely, although not altogether, on intellectual and economic snobbery. I knew that I was in equal parts appalled and gratified that my elder daughter's religious preference ran at present to para-ecclesiastical groups on her college campus.

Being remarkably slow-witted in social situations, however, I never got this said to my friend that evening. Actually I do my most incisive, logical debating while I am weeding the garden. It was the next day before I straightened out in my mind why a Hare Krishna child would be less satisfying to me as one who had fulfilled her destiny. Yes, while that sort of religious searching, that taking up of an unusual sect, would show a seriousness of purpose, it also would be, to some extent, faddish, as my friend had declared. But that part was negligible. I had had my fling with fads too. But whatever psychosocial worth was to be found in other "world religions," and they are many, I would never see them as fulfilling my children's ultimate destiny. These religions are indeed to be valued and respected. They organize life so that what is human, the spirit, is not altogether lost and devalued. They keep alive the hunger for, and even the taste of, God. They contain much more wisdom and truer psychological insights than one finds in western technology and the reduced sense of humanity it has produced. The sayings of Confucius are infinitely more valid than those of B. F. Skinner. If I had to choose between my child's being a Buddhist or a behavioral scientist, I would definitely choose the former.

Still, wisdom and tranquillity and temple bells and mendicants do not adequately reveal the whole of our destiny. Because they are a step above the rather primitive materialism of our own culture, they have tremendous attraction for a generation of starved spirits. We should not be surprised at college sophomores shaving their heads and begging in airports. They are having their first taste of something beyond dirt bikes and dope. And when one first learns that life is indeed more than food and raiment, the discovery can be intoxicating.

But no, I argue with my absent friend as I pull pigweed out of the beans, it's more than just a matter of family tradition. I don't want my daughters to be Christians just because our family always has been, albeit somewhat haphazardly. And I'd certainly be fooling myself if I thought that would be a convincing reason for them. I want their experience of the holy to be more than merely the collecting of spiritual antiques. The initial discovery, whether through exotic cult or ancestral denomination, that they have souls may be a start, but it's not the same as fulfilling their destiny. The intended destiny of every person is Christ. That goes beyond wisdom and tranquillity to crucifixion and resurrection.

Nevertheless, though I do not see myself as transmitting the Christian faith as a matter of cultural obligation, I do recognize the need to transmit it, to teach it, *somehow*. My own faith is so intertwined with my early learning that I cannot imagine the sort of creature I would be today without it. Bible stories structured my personality from the start. Abraham was hardly older or more distant than my grandfather. The good Samaritan lived on my block. The Jordan River rolled through Walker County and angels hovered over my bed at night. God loving me was no harder to understand than my mother's lap. I ate and breathed Scripture as easily and unconsciously as kids do Sesame Street today.

But I face a different kind of world now. When I teach American literature to college students, I have to explain who Noah was. Allusions to the Promised Land go right past them. Their own culturally shared references are rapidly replaced media figures. They recognize Mork and Mindy, but Howdy Doody has already faded from common memory.

This then is our dilemma: how to transmit faith from one generation to the next without falsifying it as a mere cultural appendage, the icing on the cake of Americanism, a family idiosyncrasy like a preference for crunchy or smooth peanut butter. For the fact that God's revelation of himself transcends any culture, including ours, does not negate the human act of passing on our spiritual heirloom, the pearl of great price.

Our dilemma is complicated by the fact that little of anything is being transmitted generationally any more. No folklore, no salty bits of proverbial wisdom, not even the family farm. Even if the old homeplace is inherited, it is soon sold off because that spot and its memories are now meaningless to the next generation. In fact, as Margaret Mead has pointed out, the younger generation must today instruct their elders in how to live in the modern world. Skills the grandparents may have laboriously developed over decades are now obsolete. No one needs to know how to plow a straight furrow or what charm to say when you churn to make the butter come.

This stigma of superfluous knowledge attaches indiscriminately to all things old-fashioned. We have a surprisingly uncritical arrogance toward the past. "Tradition" has become a bad word. We claim to know more than our ancestors, and in that we may be correct. That does not necessarily mean that we know better.

It is only when we become parents, and especially when we become parents of teenagers, that we begin to question our own

built-in obsolescence. As Christians we long, yearn, grow frantic to
instill the faith in our children. But how? Is it possible any longer?
Have we set ourselves an impossible task? Where have we gone
wrong? We look back at our own parents, and suddenly the perspective has changed. We can see now what they were trying,
however ineptly, to do. How they were trying to articulate their
knowledge of God to us.

Are we failing? Have we failed? Are these generational
abysses new? Is there any instruction or solace from the past? Have
other fathers and mothers, sons and daughters, suffered these same
separations? What honest hope can be found in their stories? Can
we really believe in the return of the prodigal? Does the transmission of faith ever transcend the stultifying familiarity of parental
platitudes?

On an even deeper level, we are terrified by prophecies of
the disintegration of the family as a basic unit of human identity.
All we know about ourselves is suddenly called into question, for
families are the means by which human beings know themselves
—what they are now, how they got that way, and what they are
expected to become. Without them we are adrift with no means of
establishing an identity, a self. Even rebels must have a point of
reference, something to rebel against. Becoming a human being,
wrestling our amorphous and inarticulate hungers and possibilities
into shape, almost any shape, can only be accomplished by being
surrounded by examples of that process in various stages of
production—siblings and cousins both younger and older, grandparents left alone or in pairs, aunts and uncles either single or
married, and especially fathers and mothers. Not to live inside this
animated gallery of instructive models is to suffer deprivation so
deep that one's identity as human becomes deformed or severely
limited. Indeed, whether such a one could actually conceive of
himself as a person is doubtful. Even Romulus and Remus, the
legendary founders of Rome, and Mowgli, Kipling's jungle child,
were adopted into wolf *families*.

Most of the world's storytelling, from Adam and Eve to
"Eight is Enough," is devoted to family sagas. Greek tragedies
chronicle both the durability and failure of families. Centuries
before Freud, they probed the limits of human relationships with

Oedipus, Electra, Antigone and Medea. Our own current popular drama does the same with the Bunkers, the Waltons, the Sanfords, the Jeffersons, the Kintés of "Roots," and all those stress-ridden generations of "As the World Turns." Family has always been our way of explaining us to ourselves.

And family is also the Bible's way of explaining not only us, but God, and our relation to him and to one another. Our most important metaphor for God is Father. Few of us have ever known, directly, a king. Or a feudal lord. Or even a shepherd. But we all know, firsthand, parents. And we have all been, without exception, children. It is in this context that we have our earliest and most abiding experience of God, a strange union of the most common and accessible human experience coupled with the most elevated and divine. Most of us at some point even come to be both children and parents simultaneously, thus adding the deepest dimension to our understanding of the mystery that is God in three persons.

Nor can we change the metaphors without changing the meaning. We cannot disavow our heavenly Father without doing damage to our own identity as his children, both individually and communally. To turn human experience metaphorically into a cosmic day-care center is to put an agonizing distance between us and our spiritual source; we put ourselves in danger of becoming autistic and isolated.

In such a world as ours, where extended clans have shrunk to nuclear families and are now being further subdivided into single-parent families, where children are abused and abandoned, and where grandparents are stored in nursing homes, we would do well to explore more deeply the receding richness of this familial imagery, to remind ourselves of our relatives, both human and divine. This feast of families is not all sweetness, certainly. There is a good deal of saltiness and a rather large portion of bitterness— beginning with Cain and Abel. But families, in the midst of a depressing selection of artificial substitutes, continue to have the taste of reality. They tell us about our real predicament, even when we don't like what we hear.

What follows is not a plan for protecting Christian families from insidious influences. It is neither strategy nor instruction, simply because my own investigation of family sagas proves, if anything, that life is simply too unwieldy and unexpected to be managed into tidy self-help manuals. Indeed, if it were predictable enough to be packaged, the very concepts of destiny and grace would themselves disappear. Instead, what follows are stories of families struggling to transmit an old, old story. There are monumental failures among them, at least when seen from our temporal perspective. And there are incredibly sweet successes, or, more accurately, amazing amounts of grace.

CHAPTER ONE

Going Home Again

At least once a year I make a fifteen hundred mile trip home to visit my family. Of course, like almost every other adult, I use that word *family* in at least two different ways. There is the family I chose to help create. It is made up of myself, my husband, and our two daughters. We would also probably include the dog that has been with us for half of our twenty-two years. That family is "my" family in the sense that I chose it, brought it into being, and have helped to shape it, for good or ill. To some extent it is my work and artifact. It is the family in which I am parent.

But the family in which I am child is another story. My

relation to it is exactly the reverse. I had nothing to do with its creation. Indeed, in that circle it is I who am the artifact. That family is a part of the "given" of my world. Its members are there the way sun and oxygen are there. They include not only my mother and father and brother but grandparents, two generations of aunts and uncles, and an assortment of cousins.

One must have something in this world to take for granted—or "granite" as children sometimes say—and they are my granite, my bedrock. This original family of mine provides me with a broad and steady base to stretch out on.

So, like a pertinacious paleontologist, I take these trips home at least partially to chip away at this bedrock and discover fossilized clues about my own origin and evolution. Families always watch themselves for duplicated noses, a similar timbre in voices, or even recurrent patterns in child rearing. But this trip I am after different quarry. It is not just inherited physiognomy or imbedded social behavior that I'm looking for. My search is for signs of a shared spirituality. A way of seeing life and striking terms with it that will be traceable through at least three, maybe four, generations.

Families are not just the product of a certain limited genetic pool or of economic and political forces. They are themselves units of human meaning. And that meaning they carry as certainly as chromosomes has been subjected every day, year in and year out, to stress. Somewhere in their past, all American families have had to cope with famine, religious scruples, slavery, or conquest. Such stress shapes and stretches the family faith just as it alters physical traits. Sometimes the inherited spirituality collapses, just as genetic pools dry up and family lines die out. When Jesus said, "Nevertheless, when the Son of Man comes, will he find faith on the earth?" he was not asking a rhetorical question.

All of us who claim to have faith received that gift from someone. For most of us that someone was a family member. The actual content of that faith, the breath of the Spirit itself, comes only from our heavenly Father. But the shape that faith takes in us, the receptacle in which we hold the gift, is a product of human enterprise. The Psalms, for example, the oldest heirlooms in human history, have descended to us over the centuries because they were handed down from generation to generation as the shape of a shared spirituality. They shaped the Israelites coming out of Egypt; they shape me sailing at thirty thousand feet toward Texas. They have survived the stress of exile, war, poverty, famine, death, and dispersion. Can they survive the stress of my own century?

I look out the plane window as it cruises through clouds whipped up from the Gulf coast. When I was a child, clouds were a matter of magic. Literally, their matter was magical, different from earthbound stuff. Like huge barges of raw cotton they floated down the sky, their mystery enhanced by the possibility of their harboring angels. My childish fancy was shared by the psalmist. For him Jehovah rode the storm clouds surrounded by the hosts of heaven. Now we fly over or through these imagined habitations of heavenly beings and I discover firsthand that they are mist. On their own terms, these shifting vapors are as fascinating as their displaced cottony images, but in some way my private insight into the life of the spirits has been stressed by this discovery. I have had to readjust my expectations or my faith would have come crashing down out of the clouds.

If this same experience is multiplied to include several generations, what happens? It is only in my lifetime that any member of our family has flown through clouds. Does that kind of experience cause a spiritual dislocation severe enough to make all the stores of the past of no account? Is it necessary to start over again on the spiritual enterprise because of airplanes? Should I make a clean swipe of the slate and scrap the treasures of my faith? Can I still speak the same spiritual language with my relatives?

It is not just a matter of clouds, of course. Not many miles from the runway where my plane will land is the control center that guides astronauts and satellites among the stars. Space flight rearranges our whole notion of the universe, and of ourselves. It can make us feel simultaneously insignificant and arrogant. Any change in our picture of the outside world causes a corresponding change in our interior world and puts a new stress on the link to the past.

In their early years my older earthbound kinfolks' travel was limited to mule-drawn wagons. Does this limit also their experience of life an death? Has their research into the essential questions been faulty and their information inadequate? Is there anything from the days of their lives worth preserving or is their experience best sloughed off like an outgrown skin?

The question cuts two ways. Not only do I have to consider what of value I have inherited from them. I also have to face the possibility of my own spiritual obsolescence. Has it been worth my while to store up heavenly treasure for my children, or will they find my faith unequal to the unforeseen stresses the future will put on their lives?

There are, after all, people like Margaret Mead who say generational roles must be reversed now; that in a technological society with its rapid explosion of knowledge the old must learn from the young. My own fascination for the past is not common even in my own family. Until my generation, both sides of my family were without exception agriculturally based. None of them, since they came to this continent, had lived in cities. They either inherited the family farm or married into other farming families. When they migrated westward, it was to continue the same way of making a living they had always known. But with World War II my parents' generation starting leaving the farm. Now almost all my cousins live in cities. They work for insurance companies, own automobile dealerships, sell business machines. They are thoroughly enmeshed in technological society. None of the skills by which they earn their living were known to my grandparents. And none of the skills by which my grandparents survived—growing their own food, building their own homes, making their own clothes—are important enough in the modern world to take any pains to preserve.

Typical is a cousin who works as an engineer, a long way from home. His parents have little notion of what his work is. And he, for his part, has long since discarded the family faith. It was like a vaccination that didn't take. Or perhaps the virus it was intended to guard him against is now an entirely new strain. At any rate, like me, he lives several states away from home now. He has relocated, not only physically but spiritually.

Change swirls us about so rapidly that even the last decade's way of understanding life seems dowdy and out of date. A decade now accomplishes what a century used to. Energy exploration, population control, genetic engineering, information retrieval systems, artificial intelligence modes. Compared to these, salvation seems esoteric, a quaint hobby. Even the terminology sounds archaic. Our age has learned to update the old straightforward spiritual epithets with words like "self-fulfillment."

Still, I need to know if those ancestors who are yet within my grasp have anything to tell me. I don't want the hard-won truth of their lives to be buried and lost under the accreted strata of technological ages. I must discover whether they have anything to teach me in order to know if *I* will have any significance to the future. I want to unpack a few trunks of ancestral treasures, to hold the heirlooms up to the light and finger the fabric for flaws, for durability and workmanship.

"One generation shall laud thy works to another" was the formula prescribed by the psalmist. "They shall abundantly utter the memory of thy great goodness." The method and rationale for maintaining Jewish tradition is constantly repeated in the Psalms. "Things that we have heard and known, that our fathers have told us. We will not hide them from our children, but tell to the coming generation. . . . that the next generation might know them, the children yet unborn, and arise and tell them to their children, so that they should set their hope in God, and not forget the works of God, but keep his command. . . ." By these means the children of Abraham have survived into the twentieth century.

For four thousand years the Jews have used this means of maintaining their spiritual identity. One of the most sacred duties commanded by the Torah is the teaching of religion to one's children. In the early days of Israel's history, one's immortality was reckoned in the continued faithfulness of one's offspring. Abraham lived again in each new generation, and it was thus that God's promise to him would be fulfilled. The Gospel of Matthew itself begins, "A record of the genealogy of Jesus Christ the son of David, the son of Abraham." Then follows the listing of forty-two generations tracing Jesus as Abraham's descendant. Obviously the unbroken line of tradition was just as important to Matthew and his Jewish readers as was the Virgin Birth.

Unfortunately, few of us can follow the thread of our own

ancestry so successfully. And if we do undertake to trace our family tree, it is seldom for reasons that have anything to do with our spiritual heritage.

Human identity has undergone a decided shift in the modern world, one that has less and less to do with traditions of any kind. Each successive generation now feels it must start from scratch in making up the rules by which we play this game of life. Individuals must be allowed to create their own identities, unhindered by the constraints of inheritance. No information from the past about what is either helpful or hostile to human life is permitted to penetrate the present.

I have nothing in my house that belonged to my grandparents, no relic of their lives, other than a few recent photographs. My children have names that, to my knowledge, have never been used in either of their parents' families before. Yet the thought that my hypothetical grandchildren will not keep about them any of my relics is disturbing to me, not for my sake but for theirs. For I remember rainy afternoons spent with a great-aunt who kept what she called a treasure chest for my brother and me. It was full of old things—lace collars, hat pins, quilt pieces, photograph albums—which we got to handle, one at a time, and wonder about. It stirred something in us for which we as children had not even a name. I'm sure it was not merely nostalgia; the interests of children are too direct for that kind of convoluted longing. We were searching for clues to our ancestors' identity—and ours—as we hunted among the bric-a-brac in the trunk.

Almost anyone who goes home with great expectations— or great need—is in danger of intoxication from the memories that rise like mist from this specially hallowed ground. I want most strenuously to avoid nostalgia for its own sake. A quick wallow in the swamps of sentiment is not what I'm after. I admit to a longing for home, a fascination with my own early formation. But the familiar faces that were part of my childhood furniture, the favorite dishes cooked just for me, the old stories and photographs brought out again and turned over lovingly—I must look past all these, past the little waves of nostalgia that lap about the cockles of my heart, to what is really there.

Even so, dangerous as it is, I have some confidence in my

method. Paul Tournier says the simplest and most obvious thing in his book *To Understand Each Other:* "Modern psychology has taught us the decisive role played by our earliest experiences. Our lifelong attitudes to others were determined by them. Many of these events we have forgotten. It is by talking about them that reminiscences come, or even dreams which present them to us in veiled symbolism."

The plane has landed, is racing along the runway. And in a sense, my descent through the clouds has landed me in a dream. To all of us our past becomes mythological when we grow up and leave home. Perhaps that is why so many people are determined to ignore it. Myth is concentrated life; its characters are huge, larger than life. All home things are inflated with memory and meaning. And the only way of learning the truth of that dream is by walking into it wide-eyed. By going home again.

CHAPTER TWO

Born Yesterday

Jesus said we must become like children to enter the kingdom of his Father. I am never so much a child as when I come home.

Many of my friends tell me they find going home a fearful undertaking. They feel themselves sinking irresistibly into a childishness they thought they had put behind them. They watch, unnerved, as their hard-won identity as mature, responsible adults crumbles under the weight of the mythological mammoths of their past.

For my part, however, I still take delight on being fussed over—my father carrying my bags, the rose that is waiting on my desk, the breakfast made for me every morning. These few weeks of escape from responsibility may be regression, but I enjoy every indulged minute of it.

In the autumn afternoon I whistle the dogs with me into the woods and sit on a log to do nothing but watch the light change. No one is depending on me to do anything today. All I have to do is be.

Have you forgotten? This is the way life was when you were very young. This is the sort of creature Jesus stood in the midst of his disciples for an example. Be like this, he said. And no doubt the child turned and looked up at his face in order to catch the glint of meaning there in the way children do when they're unable to understand the words. What *was* he trying to tell us?

I sit on the log, not trying to make anything happen, just watching the light fall. Isn't this what intrigues us so much in those photographs of children's faces we see on television or in ·magazines, even children in the midst of famine and war? They are just watching things happen, whether it's light or kingdoms falling around them.

It's only momentarily, sitting alone on logs, that we can recapture that way of being. The faces of adults in those same critical situations look quite different. Frowning, resolute, concerned, anguished. They are all trying to do something about their peril, something noble or something self-serving. But they have all passed beyond that steady, waiting gaze of childhood.

I have a private game to amuse myself in public places. I watch the faces of strangers in airports, restaurants, shopping malls, street corners, and try to imagine what they looked like as children. The challenge seems especially great with men. Could I match that bushy-browed bald head with his second-grade class picture? Would he be the one with the incorrigible cowlick? Was his smile shy? Or was his chin lifted in a cocky challenge to the world? At what point did he gain that self-assured hanging jowl? That managerial arch of the eyebrow?

What would it do to people if they were required to carry around, like an open locket, their grade school picture for all to see and compare what was promised with what has been delivered? The fact that our offspring find most incredible about us is that we were ever children.

My parents' walls are covered with photographs of my brother and me from our early years. In some way they are a reproach. My own face will never be that open again. In all the later pictures a veil has descended. There is a guardedness, a cautiousness, a consciousness of presenting oneself to the world. I'll never see with those eyes again—the eyes that are letting the Christmas tree happen, that are beholding the birthday party come down as complete as the New Jerusalem from heaven. But those are the eyes that see the kingdom of heaven, says Jesus. How, oh how, do we regain that sight?

It is a mighty question. One on which our salvation hangs. That little interlude about the kingdom belonging to children recorded by Matthew, Mark, and Luke is not a mere bit of sentimental fluff, a scriptural children's hour. In John's gospel Jesus puts it even more strongly; he tells Nicodemus he must be born again. Unfortunately we've turned the phrase into a brand name for Christianity instead of taking the instruction seriously.

It's strange that we should have so often failed to connect the two commands: to become like children and to be born again. But what other means could give us back those eyes, that face, except such a radical reversal? For rebirth is not the same as reformation. A little cosmetic surgery won't do. Rebirth is not a bad man becoming good or a good man becoming better. The demands are much more dreadful and drastic than that.

In the end it will be fruitless for us to try to transmit faith to our children unless we have ourselves entered the dark and fertile womb of the Spirit where all our well-guarded adult prerogatives are undone, where all our faded perceptions of the world disintegrate. This is the part we don't like, nor it seems did Nicodemus. One can hear the revulsion in his voice as he shudders at entering a second time into his mother's womb. Adults pride themselves on not being taken in—there are so few consolations to maturity. To us, the warm, close, sheltering dark is the definition of a prison. Freud made quite a lot from that fear.

But those are the conditions of rebirth. The death and disintegration of the failed self we have been laboriously constructing for years. All the education, all the character building, all the rules for right and rewardable behavior, all the careful and prudent planning, all the methods for successfully manipulating life must first dissolve in the austere amniotic fluid of the Spirit. And only then does a little cluster of cells begin to take shape.

Once again, sentiment too often traps us when we recall Jesus' teaching about becoming a child. All the rosy notions of childhood peculiar to our century were certainly not shared by first century Galilee. The disciples were probably dumbfounded by their rabbi's setting a child in their midst for their edification. Perhaps they took it as another of his whims, like looking at lilies or cursing barren fig trees. Still, someone remembered and wrote it down. There it sits on the page. And we've been trying for centuries to figure out just what it means. We try to assume what we take to be the various postures of childhood. We call these Innocence, or Trust, or Simple Faith. I suspect, however, that those who actually have become like children, like children don't spend much time thinking about it.

But if that saying does nothing else for us, it keeps us from dismissing childhood as spiritually insignificant. We have grown a little leery lately of youthful conversions. Children, we think, don't know enough of the world, haven't adequate information or the ability to make high-level abstractions necessary to decisions about something as awesome as eternity. They haven't hit the hard stuff yet. Maybe. But it may be also that we've forgotten how expansive, how vast the world was to our early eyes, those eyes that see the Kingdom.

Although my Bible stories were absorbed with no chronological discrimination—Abraham mixed with the Good Samaritan, Paul in prison alongside the Tower of Babel—they were a good deal more real to me than to most adults who have them stored safely in history. And when I rose, dripping and smelling slightly of chlorine, from the baptistry on my eighth Easter and hurriedly shivered into my new navy blue suit and red blouse spattered with white birds, my imaginative grasp of new life in Christ was at least equal to that of the adults I see furtively approaching the font today.

G. K. Chesterton and John Henry Cardinal Newman were both adult Roman Catholic converts. There the similarity stops. Chesterton was a rotund, burly extrovert while Newman was a careful, analytic ecclesiastic. Except for one thing. Their childhood visions. In his autobiography Chesterton savors his first visual impression, that of a swaggering young man wearing a gold crown and a curly moustache, carrying a large gold key and crossing a bridge to a castle. The figure, it turns out, was no more than a cardboard character in a toy theater built by his father. Nevertheless, it was a peculiarly compelling picture, for he hoarded it over a period of spiritually impoverished years until the "overwhelming conviction that there is one key that can unlock all doors" brought back to him this "first glimpse of the glorious gift of the senses. . . . And there starts up again before me," he declares, "the figure of a man who crosses a bridge and who carries a key. . . ."

Newman too begins his autobiography with what he selects as his "most definite" early memory. "I used to wish the Arabian Tales were true: my imagination ran on unknown influences, on magical powers, and talismans. I thought life might be a dream, or I an Angel, and all this world a deception, my fellow-angels by a playful device concealing themselves from me, and deceiving me with the semblance of a material world." Plato himself couldn't have put it better, this reality invisible to the veiled vision of maturity. What comes awkwardly to us comes effortlessly to these new creatures who still have eyes to see.

When a child, after bedtime stories of danger and deliverance, asks that inevitable question (one that never ceases to disconcert adults), "Is it true?" what he means is: "Is that the way the world really is?" Are Lassie and Black Beauty and Rebecca of Sunnybrook Farm a part of the structure of reality? Can I count on the consolation of the final Happy Ending? Will virtue be ultimately rewarded and evil made of no account? Children hunger and thirst after righteousness with a much finer palate than their jaded parents.

It was the *story* of Jesus that lured my heart down the aisle on a Sunday morning, not any well-reasoned argument of his existence. Children, of necessity, must suffer fools gladly, and I only stared as the minister tried to explain the economics of the Atonement. At any rate, it was Lassie and Black Beauty and all the Little Women who descended into the baptismal waters with me, there to be redeemed by the Sacrifice at the center of the world, the

Hero who holds all things together and who makes all other deeds of valor true.

"There is no other tale ever told that men would rather find was true," Tolkien says of the great eucatastrophe of the gospel. I suspect that make-believe has more uses than childish amusement. Certainly it did for Chesterton and Newman, and for me. It is neither archaeology nor scholarship that engenders our will to believe, to make belief, but the profound satisfaction and relief as the Story slips securely into that truth-shaped hole in the middle of us. Unfortunately, by the time we get to be adults, we have squirreled away so many broken fragments of things we take for truth that the Story has a hard time finding room in us.

So to all the other meanings we suspect in Jesus' command to become like children, I add my own unshakable loyalty to that small figure resplendent in her new baptismal clothes. Not because of her superior innocence. Morality has little to do with it. But because her sense of life is larger than mine. I expect too little; she expects everything. Nothing is too good to be true. After all, it is the old Nicodemus in all of us who asks Jesus, "How can these things be?"

"I can only say," writes Chesterton as he concludes his youthful reminiscence, "that this nursery note is necessary if all the rest is to be anything but nonsense. . . . In the chapters that follow, I shall pass to what are called real happenings, though they are far less real." Grown-ups use the term the "real world" to mean that sad realm of disappointed hopes and compromised dreams, thereby affirming their belief in the Fall, if not the Redemption. In that "real world" one makes jokes about happy endings. To entertain playful angelic powers is madness. That is why any entrance into the reality of redemption must be made through that make-believing child we all once were.

The light is still falling through the trees, bringing a few leaves down with it. The dogs nudge me with their noses to make sure I'm awake and aware of the time. So, having watched the woods happen for one afternoon, we go back to the house where my father has the teapot waiting for me. He looks such a pleased and happy child, making a tea party for a little girl in a red, birded blouse.

CHAPTER THREE

The Home Folks

Like a historian investigating Stonehenge, one goes home to examine relics. The monuments are the old folks, the generation that is passing away, moving beyond us, receding from our vision. They loom larger than our parents, are more mythical, because their loss is imminent. Of that generation, there are four left for me to see: my grandfather and grandmother and two great-aunts. The youngest among them is seventy-eight. They stand like the monoliths at Stonehenge, difficult to decipher now, but imbedded deep in the imagination.

These four are the remaining relics of a world already gone. On television there are no stereotypes that match them. They do not have a lifestyle. Their identity is not in crisis. Solzhenitsyn has complained that the West produces no more interesting personalities, and for the most part I agree with him. Except for these four. They have been and still are capable of acts, thoughts, words, beliefs—all innocent and unconscious—that outrage and overwhelm the rest of their family.

Perhaps the stronger flavor of their personalities comes from the deeper texture of their lives. Compared to theirs, my life has come to me filtered and refined of its rawer sensory elements. Slaughtering hogs in the keen November frosts, washing newborn babies, tending to death in the downstairs bedroom, digging sweet potatoes from the damp sand at dawn, lighting kerosene lamps at dusk—the sheer physical depth of their lives has been many times richer than the stainless-steel smoothness of mine.

One has to find a way of talking to them that takes account of this difference. Ask them if their existence is meaningful and their personalities fulfilled and you'll get a blank stare for your impertinence. Ask them if they're saved and you'll get a straight and succinct answer. How you interpret it is your business.

Going home always means at least one meal eaten in each of their homes. Not to eat at the table of one's kin is tantamount to refusing an invitation to the messianic banquet. Even when we have nothing to say to one another, even if conversation is impossible, we always manage to eat together.

"Food is love," I used to say with an edge of sarcasm when explaining my family's rituals. I don't know what else I expected it to be. Today we like to picture our essential selves as wraithlike creatures too fine for the comforts of common carnivores. But better love as food than love as emotion. It has a firmer root in Scripture and a steadier grip on reality. Jesus knew this when he fed his followers that ultimate supper.

And my grandmother knows it too. The next noon I find myself sitting down to a dinner it would have taken me two days to prepare, all fixed that morning by Granny hobbling around the kitchen in her aluminum walker. I know the dishes well. They haven't changed much over the years, although other things have. There was a time when candle moths, attracted by the kerosene lamps, flopped limply in the gravy. Today Granny cooks on an electric stove and we eat beef from the supermarket.

After a hard life of field work and raising eleven children, she's delighted by modern gadgetry, chief of which she considers a small electric organ. She has learned to pick out on it a selection of hymns and gospel songs, the most recognizable being "The Old Rugged Cross" and "Just As I Am." It gives her afternoons a solitary delight.

Indeed her capacity for enjoyment has expanded enormously in her last decade. The reasons for this are concrete and simple. She, unlike her friends in the World War I Veterans Auxiliary, still has her husband. Also, her children shower her with electrical gifts—can openers, blankets, hair dryers, crockpots. They write her letters and send her yearly school pictures of grandchildren and great-grandchildren which she arranges in little shrines around the living room.

As a child I feared her as a hard and merciless woman. I have seen her beat her two youngest sons, both in high school then, with a wet rope. She claimed to have seen Jesus thirty years ago during an electrical storm on a backwoods farm. But all the hard edges of bitterness that come from years of brutalizing work and isolation have melted from her now. Her topknot is tidier than ever, her little gray moustache is softened by a benign and constant smile.

She leads a life of private but voluble devotion supported by her organ and the radio. My grandfather, who had a falling out with her somewhat exotic denomination several years ago, refuses to drive her any more to its lone outpost thirty miles away. But Granny is a great believer in wifely submission, and being married to a stubborn man gives more scope for exercising this virtue.

I help her spread the feast on the checkered oilcloth, and we all sit down. My grandfather takes a deep breath and plunges into the grace. He asks the blessing at meals more in the tone of a tenant farmer giving due recognition to the rights of the landholder than as a child giving thanks to a generous and loving father. He tacitly acknowledges that he has no claim to the gifts we are about to receive and that indeed all mankind is undeserving of bounty, but it goes against his grain to accept even God's charity.

All the good stories my grandfather tells take place in the past when the black, east Texas dirt grew cotton so high one year he could ride his horse under the arches formed between the rows. When even the dread of the Depression was not enough to make him take a job as a revenuer to scout out his neighbors' stills. When he laid railroad ties in France to save democracy. When he had his tonsils taken out in a barber's chair and walked five miles home in the heat afterward. When he, a Texas tenant farmer, stood up to anything a harsh world sent his way and survived.

Survival is his story, but one that seems to have diminishing returns. At eighty-three he has buried six brothers and sisters, one wife, and three children. He does it with the grim satisfaction of a true stoic. His most significant social organization is not the church but his World War I veterans group, which, since his friend George moved to Florida, consists only of himself and the widows in the auxiliary. He is coming to question the ultimate value of survival.

The closer they get to the present, the sadder the stories become. The man on the neighboring farm has just killed himself because he had cancer. All his friends are dying or having strokes and going to nursing homes. His children move to other states and rarely eat at his table any more. Those are the sad facts of the life of a survivor. But he asks no quarter and seeks no heavenly comfort.

He says to me after dinner, "I've always tried to find something funny about every situation, no matter how sad and sorry." But his jokes are often bitter these days. Still, this is the way he fends off tragedy. He will not allow his heart to be broken.

He goes about his business in immaculate khakis and his red pickup which he drives with the right wheels off the pavement so he can feel where he is. Every year there is an encounter with the government over whether his license will be renewed. He knows he's losing ground with each skirmish. While he was building his last house two years ago, he cut off a couple of inches of finger which he carried to the doctor wrapped in his handkerchief and had stitched back on. He drove himself there in his pickup, of course. Until a few years ago he stood squared and upright. Now he has begun to sag in the middle like a punched sack of flour.

The virtues he admires are hard work, honesty, keeping your word, minding your own business and not meddling in other people's, self-sufficiency, firmness, unswerving loyalty, shrewdness, courage in leadership. Whatever charity he practices he keeps to himself and performs from a sense of noblesse oblige.

When he was sixty, he felt survival had its rewards. Now in his eighties he's not so sure. He's played strictly by the rules, but the game hasn't been worth the candle. He knows this, but he's not complaining. It is this very refusal to buckle under that he is relying on now to make him superior to his suffering. And to whomever is causing it. *He* is not responsible for the arrangement of the world, he seems to say. He is a Job who hasn't yet heard the voice from the whirlwind.

If anything in the church's arsenal makes sense to him, it is the doctrine of the Atonement. He knows from his own hard experience that someone always has to pay. And often the strong have to pay for the weak. That's the way things are. His personal devotion to Christ resides in his admiration for his bravery in facing the cross. Again, noblesse oblige.

He has not gone to church for many years now, except for funerals. There is a certain softness about contemporary religion that does not suit his style at all. If he has never been violent, like my grandmother, neither can he now be gentle. A stoic cannot afford either extreme. And if his understanding of redemption is closer to a prison parole than glory, I have to admit that he has a mighty firm grip on the doctrine of the Fall. His own experience of life has taught him to watch for unending variations on the theme of original sin. He neither shrinks from the fact that the heart of man is desperately wicked nor allows it to overwhelm him as he waits for that vindicating voice from the whirlwind to explain itself.

Another afternoon, and I sit with my widowed great-aunt Mayflower on her east verandah, screened and shuttered now against mosquitoes and the weather. This is an old house that has sheltered various branches of her family in the past, including the orphaned children of her sisters and brothers and daughter. My mother lived here when her own mother died. I spent my own first four years, which coincided with World War II, in her house.

This is what I mean by there being no modern molds to match these monoliths. By the world's reckoning, my aunt has always been a dependent woman. She has never held a paying job. She cannot drive an automobile. Her life has been consumed with cooking, cleaning, and caring for the infirm and dying, for men and children.

She also stands up in church on Wednesday night to protest what she perceives as the improvident planning of the board of deacons. She sings aloud on airplanes about the everlasting arms in order to steady the nerves of the timorous stranger in the next seat. During her frequent stays in the hospital, she checks on the home situations of her roommates to make sure they'll have adequate care when they are released. If she's not settled in her mind about it, she calls their relatives to make sure they know their duties. (Unlike her brother, my grandfather, she does not shrink from tidying up other people's business a bit.) Sometimes she has to set off down the dirt road in front of her house in the twilight to find her disoriented, half-dressed brother-in-law who lives across the road but doesn't always remember where he is.

Having survived Darwinism, desegregation, and the death of husband and child, she is undismayed by the modern world. But her brown eyes are bright with grief as she turns to tell me how she still goes out of a morning to the pasture and calls and whistles for her husband, just as she did for over fifty years, until her breath and sorrow are exhausted.

She is seventy-nine and as much a child as I ever hope to meet. Whatever is most obvious is what she does. There is never a moment's hesitation or calculation about her. When we were just married, she asked my husband, her eyes wide with innocence, if he were ever troubled with lice in his beard.

Yesterday we took her on a picnic to a nearby lake. She despises picnics, but she was glad for the outing and noticed everything—boys and dogs playing Frisbee, the paddleboats on the lake, a young family camping close by with a crying baby. She waddled off across the dark carpet of fallen leaves, her top-heavy round body tilting dangerously from side to side on her stiff little legs, to find out why the baby was crying. She came back knowing how long the couple had been married, where they lived, what they did for a living, that this was their first child and that she had colic. Of course they had been benefited by her own private remedy for colic. When we finally packed up our picnic and pulled away, the camping couple waved and smiled.

My great-aunt is an anomaly in our world, and I'm glad she lives in a tiny country community that still tolerates anomalies. But I also feel an urgency about this relic of another world—not for her sake certainly, but for mine. When she dies, where will the salt for this world come from?

We sit on the verandah watching the pecans plop onto the grass at intervals while she tells over her sorrow at her brother-in-law having to go to a nursing home in town. "It wouldn't have happened in my day, the way things used to be," she says.

In that world, charity meant meals cooked, orphans taken under one's roof, old people washed and set out in the sun every morning. In her day, even the poor, perhaps especially the poor, had opportunity for charity. No one had to attend a workshop to learn either warmth and affection or how to bury the dead and grieve for them. No wonder this ingenuous old woman can speak so directly and disconcertingly, can come so quickly to the point. But when she's gone, who will leaven the lump?

Another afternoon, another house, another dinner, another monument visited. This time I am stunned by what I find. My maiden great-aunt, at eighty-three, is unable any longer to replenish the destroyed cells of her body. It is simply grinding to a halt. She has been dying for years it seems, cell by cell, the hard way. The pigment in her eyes has faded to a cloudy gray-green. The skin covering her bones is yellow and crackled like the skin of chicken feet. The slightest pressure leaves bruises, the broken blood visible beneath the skin. Her knees are twice as big as her thigh and leg bones, and the joints in her hands are swollen and twisted. There are grainy, dried secretions around her eyelids, and her hair is lank and spare.

Every morning her oldest niece washes her and rubs lotion into her dying skin. She also dresses the terrible bedsores—raw flesh exposed for an area the size of an apple. The skin will never heal over these wounds again, but they are kept clean and free of infection.

Her spine, bent for seventy years with scoliosis, is now further contorted by a mass growing in one side of her abdomen. With medical irony they call it benign. It is a pitiful body, a dried-up hull of what it was even in its best days.

In those best days, this body's being was focused in the hands. Long and nimble, they made furniture, fixed most things that broke, did fine tailoring, and whirled a deft tatting shuttle to make lace edgings for pillowcases. She was an expert craftsman with a profound impatience for imperfection.

Despite the shock of the bedsores, I feel not the slightest revulsion toward this body. Whatever its state, it is hers who expended the whole maternity of her nature on other people's children. When my father's mother died not long after his birth, this aunt took on the task of rearing him and his two sisters. Later she lived in our home and took care of my brother and me. But what must it be for her, such a fastidious perfectionist, to still inhabit such a derelict ruin? I think she drifts in and out of it, like water washing in and out of a hidden cove.

The worst of the destruction is the damage to her speech by pinpoint strokes, tiny explosions of blood vessels in the brain. Nothing in her seems to give way massively. Only by one string at a time is she unraveled. I sit beside her while she washes in and out, hoping it will not be long until the final string is loose and she drifts free and away from this mooring.

It is obvious I will not be able to talk to her much. What strength she has for difficult and labored articulation is spent on the ritual questions and answers about the welfare of each family member. The slurred speech is a burden for us both.

These afflictions in the brain, whether caused by bursting blood or clogged arteries, seem the last device of the Devil to degrade us who are made in the image of God. What it means to the hidden lives of those it afflicts, I don't know, but it sorely tries the faith of onlookers. For us it becomes an enforced voyeurism into the desecration of a personality. What must it be like, we wonder, inside that stifled, suffocating brain where the words swirl around and only occasionally find their proper outlet?

She used to tell us stories about the lumber camps set up in the virgin timber of east Texas, about panthers that screamed in the night like women in the Big Thicket. But there will be no more stories now. The tongue that was always as nimble as the fingers, as quick and sharp as the glinting needle, is now only a slack muscle wallowing in the mouth.

My essential aunty is not very much present any more. She is slowly evaporating from this drying husk; only a little residue remains now, the merest smudge of herself to convince us of continued life. And even that bit diminishes daily. By her own request she does not go to the hospital but spends her days laid out on the sofa before the front window so she can watch the year come to an end.

The movement of the household takes place around her. Dying is installed on the sofa. Visitors will kindly take notice. A monument, a relic in its last hours among us. This is it, the monument says, teaching us to live with what we fear. This is death, decay, degeneration. Unmediated mortality. The end of all flesh. *Memento mori.* And if you can't stand the heat, get out of the kitchen.

One stands the heat by sitting there holding the twisted hand and murmuring inane remarks every few minutes, remarks that require no response, by not allowing one's distaste for a dirty death to come between oneself and whatever dregs are left in this cracked and leaking vessel.

What more remains to be said of the four monuments? Are they only markers in the graveyard of a dead age?

In Chaim Potok's novel, *My Name is Asher Lev,* the hero finds his imagination haunted by the powerful inherited memories of his ancestor. "I was told about him so often during my early years that he began to appear quite frequently in my dreams: a man of mythic dimensions, tall, dark-bearded, powerful of mind and body.... He left a taste of thunder in my mouth." Every decision that Asher Lev made about his destiny was submitted to this ancestor who stalked his subconscious dreams. He was the embodiment of a powerful religious heritage that the rebellious hero had to answer to.

Madeleine L'Engle in *The Summer of the Great-Grandmother* sought among several generations to discover what power was available to her through the lives of her own ancestors. She found that the extraordinary force of their personalities which carried them through fires, raiders, wars, floods, bereavement, isolation, and sudden poverty erected a standard of behavior that kept her upright under the blows life dealt her. They had left her a record of what human beings were capable of under adversity. She had empirical proof that bravery, fortitude, and cheerful perseverance were actual, had indeed been embodied in certain of her ancestors. And if in them, why not in her? If they could live through disasters undaunted, she reckoned she could too.

Living up to the past is an old-fashioned idea, I expect, one that most people have discarded as a means of dealing with an uncertain future. Gauged against the values of the time I live in, it seems a pointless exercise, this contriving to make a memorial out of these four old relics. I only dream I can keep their stories alive. The undeniable odds are that my private Stonehenge will inevitably be tumbled over, plowed under, and ground into the oblivious dust.

I am inclined, like the Preacher in Ecclesiastes, to say, "There is no remembrance of men of old, and ever those who are yet to come will not be remembered by those who follow." Nothing so convinces one of the vanity of human wishes as a deserted graveyard. All the contracts for perpetual care are eventually voided. Fifty years after their death, the memory of most human beings has perished from the earth.

But it is, after all, God's name that the generations exist to proclaim, not their own. Our own names, our own stories must be entrusted to a more able recorder than ourselves and our children. We know we cannot create our own immortality out of words any more than we could create our mortal selves out of dust. Human beings have this hankering to be ultimate, like God. Perhaps that is what death is meant to teach us—that we're not.

Nevertheless, we are allowed to make a mark. And these four kinfolk have marked and shaped me. Being relics of another age and to that extent mysterious, they have had a greater hold on my imagination than even my parents. Like Asher Lev's ancestor, they will stalk my memory and dreams, giving me a measure for life, a scale larger than what my own age offers. It is enough for now that I remember. The final meaning of those memories belongs to someone else.

CHAPTER FOUR

The Third and Fourth Generations

As a species we carry in our genes the potential for 1400 diseases and 120 sex-linked deficiencies. Besides that, there are independent organisms, viruses, that long ago intruded themselves into our ancestral strands of chromosomes and continue to lurk there. When these strands are divided up and passed on like heirloom pearls to the next generation, the viral interlopers stick tight as ticks and make themselves at home in the new body. Thus along with our flesh tone and blood type, our eye color and hair texture, we inherit illness. Many times the seed of what will eventually kill us is sown along with life itself—a weak heart valve, a faulty device for manufacturing thyroid molecules, an abnormal sensitivity to histamines. Supposing that we do emerge on this earth trailing Wordsworth's clouds of glory, we must also admit that they are tangled with filaments of defective, viral-infested DNA. Our conception has been somewhat less than immaculate.

Biology has been busy for the last several decades constructing a marvelous model, a compellingly apt physical analogy for the spiritual phenomenon of original sin; social scientists, on the other hand, have been just as intent on discarding the word *sin,* original or otherwise, as merely an abrupt little epithet that pretends to describe what is actually a complex social phenomenon. Susan Sontag would like to see us do away with any metaphor that links disease with moral condition.

We find ourselves, therefore, in the midst of an interesting historical paradox. Theology had long taught that human beings are linked in corruption by original sin, whereas a purblind science promoted for centuries the theory of the spontaneous generation of disease and decay. Rot and malignancy simply distilled out of the air. Surgeons coughed unabashedly on their instruments. Now biology has caught up with theology. It has discovered that disease does not simply propagate itself out of thin air. Bacilli breed from a parent cell like any other organism. But at the same time biology made this step forward, some theologians decided to scrap the notion of original sin, an actual physical chain of inherited quiet, and to put in its place biology's old superstition, spontaneous generation, cutting away this link to our ancestors. A new age, we are told, calls for a new breed. There is, however, no such thing as a *new* breed, no spontaneous generation. Only new combinations of the old components, as old as life itself. We are all of us only mutants and mongrels.

A recently developed taste for genealogy led a cousin of mine to trace my mother's family back to its appearance on this continent from Ireland and Scotland. Considering the isolation of the small agricultural communities in which they settled, it is not surprising that cousins often married cousins. When only a few families populate an entire county, there's not much matrimonial choice. Thus Sarah Proctor, an eighteen-year-old girl from the outskirts of Belfast, married her first cousin, George Adams, in 1768.

By the standards of the times, the Adamses were comfortably well-off farmers in the Carolinas, Georgia, and Tennessee. They donated land for community churches and schools. The Old Minute Book of the Mounte Zion Baptist Church of Talbot County, Georgia, shows that Sister Adams presented the congregation with vessels "for the purpose of feet washing" in 1837. Also, surprisingly enough, among the list of the church's charter members in 1835 is "Easter, a woman of color." In 1841 there is added to the roll "Isbelle, a woman of color, property of Edward Adams."

They were not, however, wealthy and did not live in pillared plantation mansions, but in decent salt-box houses with swept sand yards. Approaching death, they divided up their land and other holdings equitably among their children, each of whom also received a feather bed and furniture with which to set up housekeeping. And also at least one slave. The will of my great-great-great-grandfather William Adams made provision for his twelve children in this manner: "I also desire as my children come of age they shall have as much as I gave my son George Adams when he became of age out of my estate that is to say one Negro woman worth five hundred and fifty two dollars one horse worth sixty seven and a half dollars and one bed and cow and calf and one sow and pigs. . . ."

He was, of course, the last to make such a bequest. By the time his son, Fields Adams, died, human beings were no longer transferable property. In fact, the fortunes of this farming family fell on such unyieldingly hard times, that no wills survived after the Civil War, presumably because there was nothing left to bequeath. Fields and his son Silas came to Texas in a wagon that held the remainder of their belongings. Silas became a peddler and moved his own large family constantly from one tiny Texas town to another. His son, my grandfather, was a sharecropper cultivating other people's land. Not until he was well past his prime was he able to buy forty acres of sandy soil of his own.

As I look over these documents, compiled with pride by near and distant cousins, it is impossible to ignore the questions that form like barnacles on the nether side of the facts. Was this dispossession of a race of farmers their retribution for trafficking in human flesh? After four generations on the land which, according to their own account, the Lord their God had given them, they were forced to become wanderers across a territory at least as large as Mesopotamia, from Georgia to Tennessee to Mississippi to Texas. From their former practice of providing for the education of their many children out of their estates, they descended into several generations of ignorance and neglect of the intellect, the common curse of those who must spend every waking hour putting bread on the table for their children. And along with this default in education went a corresponding neglect of religion which was seen, and resented, as a leisure time activity. I have the testimony of one of Silas's daughters that her papa refused to go to church in town because he had only overalls to wear. When one of their daughters, who had married well, gave her a new bonnet to wear to Sunday services, my great-grandmother burned it in the kitchen stove.

Did they, any more than the Jews of the Captivity, see their dispossessed, landless state as a judgment against them? If God was responsible for their former prosperity, as they claimed, was their later dispersion a result of divine disfavor? No evidence survives that the question was ever consciously raised until my generation. Poverty goes a long way toward, if not expiating, at least taking your mind off guilt. At first they thought of themselves as victims of injustice. Later they stopped making even that historical connection. They were simply poor, like a lot of other people.

No one is bitter over what happened to the family fortunes three or four generations ago. No one asks, at least openly, if repentance would have softened the retribution. In fact, today they like to think of themselves as bootstrap pullers. But no one is sorry either for the misdeeds of those early generations. Neither the sins nor the sorrows of their fathers affect them much. Their pride lies in their survival.

In 1813, only two years before the birth of Fields Adams, the one who would bear the immediate brunt of the Civil War, a son was born to Michael Pedersen Kierkegaard in Copenhagen. Soren was the last of seven, all borne by a second wife. Whereas my family has proved almost impervious to past guilt, the Kierkegaards soaked it up like a sponge.

The story begins with no foreboding of what lay ahead for

this unfortunate family, unless one counts the curious spinal de-
formity of this youngest son, Soren. His misshapenness scarcely
seemed to matter, though, since he was the baby and the darling of
the large, prosperous, cultivated family. He was the apple of his
gifted father's eye. Their singularly active minds had a peculiar
affinity for each other. Understanding, intellectually and emotion-
ally, between the two was instantaneous.

When Soren was six, the eldest of the Kierkegaard children died in an accident. Two years later the eldest daughter died
suddenly. At about the time Soren was entering the university, his
mother died, followed quickly by three of the remaining brothers
and sisters. Only Soren, his brother Peter, and their father survived, living together steeped in melancholy in the large family
home on the main square of Copenhagen. It was then that, by
supposedly independent trains of thought, all three survivors came
to the same conclusion: the family was under a curse, a judgment
from God.

Soren's father, Michael, traced the cause of this judgment
back to a scene from his childhood when he had lived as a peasant
in the poorest district of Jutland. Sent to tend sheep on the desolate
moor, the twelve-year-old Michael, desperately lonely, had climbed
to the top of a hill, clenched his fists, raised them to the heavy sky,
and cried curses at the God who had brought him to such an
extremity.

The sky did not fall. Lightning did not strike. The sheep
went on tearing the meager grass from the sparse soil. Michael
came down from the hill and went home. And suddenly things
began to get better.

He was sent as an apprentice to a cousin's business in
Copenhagen. He learned the business easily and soon took over its
entire management. He made astoundingly successful investments
and was able to retire soon after the death of his first wife. Even
after his second marriage and the birth of seven healthy children,
his capital kept expanding. As far as money went, he could do
nothing wrong. It came to him almost unasked. And he was
friends with the most important men in Denmark. The poverty
and loneliness that had caused him to curse God on the Jutland
moor were far behind him.

But the scene on the moor was not his only dark secret. His first child, born only five months after he had married his former servant girl, was the product of seduction. Even while his first wife had lived, his sensuality had overcome his scruples in regard to the young woman under his protection.

The darkness of this guilty secret began to sap his spiritual vitality. Indeed, for many years, possibly from the time of the death of his first child, he had been prey to fits of severe melancholy which he tried desperately to hide from the rest of the family, especially his beloved Soren. But after so many deaths, after so much suffering, it became impossible to ignore. Soren himself called the revelation "the great earthquake" and described it in characteristically extreme terms:

> Then I suspected that my father's great age was not a divine blessing but rather a curse; that the outstanding intellectual gifts of our family were only given us in order that we should rend each other to pieces: then I felt the stillness of death grow around me when I saw my father, an unhappy man who was to outlive us all, a cross on the tomb of all his hopes.

So there they were, the three of them, the father and his two remaining sons, sunk in dejection in the great house in Copenhagen. Chained by cause and effect, weighed down with guilt and punishment, the father and older son accepted this construction of reality and submitted to living out the rest of their lives condemned by this "infallible law" of guilt.

Soren Kierkegaard, however, revolted. Back at the university he became the center of a political and artistic whirlwind. Burning the candle of his intellect at both ends, he challenged both the popular Hegelian philosophers and the mechanistic theology of the Danish Protestant church. He seemed intent on proving everybody wrong and, consequently, was making everyone his enemy.

It is interesting, even relieving, to note that in the midst of this student revolt, his father, unable to banish his love and care for this prodigal from his heart, rather than rebuking him or threatening to cut him out of his patriarchal bounty, instead sent him on a holiday to the coast where he would have time for reflection and restoration of his equilibrium.

And it worked for a while. But the influence of Copenhagen and university friends soon seemed to undo the good effects of the retreat. For two more years Soren noised his nihilism about, professing nothing, attacking everything. It was not until Michael, in the last year of his life, openly confessed to his son the secret sins, before only guessed at, that Soren was able finally to commit himself to what he called in his journal an "inward relation to Christianity."

But did that endlessly revolving cycle of guilt and despair end there? For the elder brother Peter it remained a lifelong burden. Even toward the end of his life, he was still under its melancholy influence and asked to be relieved of his ecclesiastical responsibilities. Soren's story is harder to discern. Betrothed to a sixteen-year-old girl, he broke off the engagement when marriage seemed imminent, despite his devotion to her the rest of her life. Was it, as he claimed, that God had vetoed the marriage, intending him for a prophet's unfettered life, one that would stir up both the political and religious establishments against him? Or was it, as he wrote elsewhere in his journal, that "I should have been compelled to initiate her into dreadful thoughts, my relation to my father, my abysmal melancholy, the eternal night which broods in my innermost being." Was he fearful also of perpetuating his father's line, opening up another channel through which God's wrath would flow? Did the knowledge of the father's sin immobilize the son's life, just as that other famous Dane, Prince Hamlet, found the conduits of his heart choked with his mother's perceived sin?

Consider Samuel Sewall, a judge in colonial New England, who was one of the special court of three commissioned to hear the evidence in the Salem witch trials of 1692. Along with the others, he condemned twenty people to death and directed that scores of others be tortured or publicly disgraced. For the next several years he struggled under the weight of what he came to acknowledge as innocent blood. On Christmas Day, 1696, he buried his little daughter. Two weeks into the new year he had a notice publicly posted in the church asking pardon of man and God for the part he had played in the Salem trials. Confession seems to have been good for Samuel Sewall's soul. Thereafter, the death of family members no longer haunted him as acts of retribution for his sin.

Like the viruses that cling to our chromosomes, guilt seems inescapable. Some people seem to throw off its effects rather easily, while others succumb to its destructive power, just as those deadly interlopers tangled in our strands of DNA break loose and kill some bodies and hibernate harmlessly in others.

I look at the scanty artifacts concerning the lives of George and Sarah, William and Susan, Fields and Elizabeth, even Easter, the woman of color and charter member of Mounte Zion Baptist Church. They are still among us in their offspring. They are still among us in ourselves, our cells. Quite literally, genetically, we are they.

Do I then feel weighed down by the guilt of my ancestors? Not particularly. Perhaps it is just that the requisite three to four generations have passed, but the tragic gloom that pervades Faulkner's South and Hawthorne's New England has dissipated. I do not expect to be exempted from whatever retribution lurks in the future, waiting to ambush us all, the natural consequences of our sin. But I do not personally feel the weight of that guilt, any more than I suffer remorse over the invasion of the Celts by the Angles and Saxons.

We are not talking here about wrong that results from our own actions and for which we feel personally responsible in our own lifetimes. Nor are we considering the salvific power of the Atonement for individuals. We are pursuing guilt on the level of the "natural" man, that unregenerate creature subject to the laws of biology and history. For even on the natural level, there seems to be a statute of limitations on guilt. Three or four generations and it is dissipated by natural processes. To pick up the genetic analogy, other chromosomes from diverse sources enter the genetic pool and bring to it fresh possibilities. It dilutes my inherited responsibility for the slaughter and dissolution of native Americans to know that my great-great-grandmother came from Cherokee stock. I am made up of both oppressors and oppressed.

Despite the viral killers clinging to our chromosomes, we're not anywhere near extinction as a species. Nor are we, as a species, driven to despair over the sins of our fathers. We're resilient. Interpose a great-grandfather between us and the sin, and we're ready to start all over again. Günter Grass, the German novelist, says his country's guilt for the Holocaust "must remain forever indelible." The God of the Holocaust victims is more merciful—and more realistic.

On the other hand, I have frequently seen Christian consciences outraged at the Old Testament prescription of three or four generations for the healing of social wounds. Individualism demands that everyone should take his own licks. But it doesn't work like that, not biologically nor historically. When I look back at my own defective ancestors, I'm grateful for the immunity those intervening generations have developed. Perhaps we should pay more attention to the mercy in the medicine.

CHAPTER FIVE

My Mother, My Sister

Every night while I am home, my mother comes into my room and sits on the side of the bed where I am propped up reading. She smoothes the sheets absently with her hand while she talks. I know that in her fastidious way she would like to round out the day by kissing me good-night, tucking me in, and turning out the light, just as she used to. Because it is only then, having finally divested herself of her duty, that she can retreat to her own room where she too reads late into the night, a solitary self alive and expanding in a pool of yellow light.

Of all the creatures in the world, mothers must bear the heaviest load of symbols. For at least 32,000 years we have been stylizing maternity. I found this out a few summers ago in San Francisco as I wandered through an exhibition of Ice Age art by the American Museum of Natural History. Among the figures of ibex and reindeer, bison and salmon, were statuettes carved in mammoth ivory or limestone representing the mythologized female. Each figurine is hung with large breasts. The hips are wide and the feet small, the knees bent slightly. The face is always featureless, most often completely smooth. Found all over Ice Age Europe, from France to the Ukraine, they have been named "Venuses" by archaeologists, somewhat inappropriately since the obvious emphasis of the artist is on their maternal function rather than the erotic. This is the one figure that appears with striking stylistic similarity in all geographic areas of Ice Age culture and from the early to the late period.

There is the black Venus of Dolni Vestonice in Czechoslovakia, perhaps 34,000 years old, with her masklike face bearing only two down-slanted eye marks. And the white ivory Venus of Lespugue, France, her bulbous breasts and hips tapering below to delicately pointed toes and above to a head well-proportioned but devoid of any features. The extremely stylized female figure carved from mammoth ivory found near Pekarna, Czechoslovakia, has only a hole where the face might have been. Though marked differences of technique and design separate the enclaves of Ice Age culture all over Europe, these female images are the one recurrent figure that appears in all of them. And though they may have elaborately carved coiffures, or wear bracelets, beads, or aprons, or even be decorated with bands of tattoos, they are always faceless.

The faceless mother. There is something at once enigmatic and unnerving about these figures, like bandits with stockings pulled over their faces. One wants to strip off the mask suddenly and surprise their identity.

Why human beings should, from earliest times, have made mother-goddesses is a mystery no anthropologist has yet explained to my satisfaction. Yet the urge to mythologize motherhood seems to have been universal. Sumerians, Egyptians, Greeks, and Romans set up shrines to this most manifest life-giver. Even the ancient Hebrews, so fiercely monotheistic and thoroughly patriar-

chal, named Eve "the mother of all living things," a title sufficient
to have made her a goddess in any other ancient culture.

I only have the muddiest notion myself about this symbol
we have defaced and called Mother. One thing I realize, though, as
I watch the hand smoothing the sheet: the content of all my primal
and most fundamental knowledge is my mother. Before I ever
opened my startled eyes on this world, all that I knew about it was
my mother—her heartbeat, her metabolism, her movement and
emotion.

When I was a child, friends and strangers alike used to
point out how much I resembled my father. The same wide
mouth, the same cleft chin. Now I am most often compared to my
mother, not, I believe, because of any structural similarity, but
because of mannerisms and facial expressions. The same way of
lifting the eyebrows or expelling a sigh.

Mother was my first knowledge of *being* itself. She was the
voice in the prenatal darkness. And later the touch. The only
world I knew for months tasted of her. Still later she became my
understanding of *how to be.* How to respond to situations. How to
decide what is valuable, admirable, fitting, proper. What is repugnant and unworthy. What to scorn and what to strive for. Even
when the outcome of my consciousness has differed from hers, the
tools for feeling out and taking in the world, the methods of
procuring and processing information, have been those she provided. I look out, look sharp, and look with my mother's eyes.

Some people find this fact distressing. Ever since Freud,
mothers have not gotten a particularly good press. Responsibility
for the foundational sins of the world has been laid in their laps.
And considering the enormous formative power they have over us,
such a judgment does seem logical. Abraham Lincoln may have
said, "All that I am or hope to be I owe to my angel mother"; but
could not Idi Amin say the same? Mothers are responsible for us.

It seems self-evident, then, that to become our "true"
selves, we must find ways of divorcing our identities, prenatally
enslaved, from those of our mothers. Everyone wants to be born
again, and this time without the interference of a mother. What we
seek is an immaculate conception of our psyches, to exist independent of reliance on someone else.

But it is not entirely modern, I think, this fear of the hand and body that feed us. The Greeks no doubt took a perverse delight in the myths of the continued humiliations of Hera, the mother goddess of their day. The violation of Jocasta, the mother and wife of Oedipus, brought about his blinding but her death. And Hamlet's feelings of shame and revulsion for his mother resulted in tragedy for both son and mother. Even Eve, the great mother of us all, has been made the scapegoat of the Fall by centuries of theologians, both Jewish and Christian. And who knows but what Mary's overthrow by the Reformers was not motivated in part by the desire to be free of any cosmic, as well as earthly, maternal influence?

Still, the fear of a suffocating maternalism, so well-documented in the history of human psychology, puzzles me when it persists past puberty. There are, of course, abberations of motherhood as with anything else in what we call the natural world. There are indeed mothers who are monsters, who try to defraud their children of their own identities. But monsters, by definition, are out of the ordinary and unrepresentative. Our own age's outcry against mothers seems out of all proportion to the probable number of mutations among us. We protest so much, I think, because we have persuaded ourselves that human beings have no business being at the mercy of anyone else's personality. We take autonomy to be ultimate. Realizing that one's identity is contingent upon some unwitting woman not of our own choosing goes against our cultural grain.

What a mother teaches so unwittingly is herself, her own being. We learn not so much *from* our mothers as we learn our mothers themselves. According to some biological experimenters, certain kinds of worms can learn by eating the ground-up bodies of a previous generation of worms who have been taught to respond to simple stimuli. This is getting close to how we come by our primal knowledge of the world—through absorption with our mother's blood.

But by what other means are we, born defenseless and naked into this world, to learn anything at all, even how to see? Independence is an absurdity for a helpless infant. Whether we like it or not, there is a point in our lives when we are totally dependent on someone else for our very survival. A puny bit of delicately structured protoplasm who has no idea of even where his fingers and toes end and the outside world begins is blissfully unaware of his dependency. It is not really accurate to say that, to an infant, the universe and he are one. For him there is only one universe, and it is he.

The difficult task of getting one's bearings in one's surroundings, indeed of discovering oneself as *one,* is mediated by the mother. Without her we are literally lost. To feel like a "motherless child" is to feel out-of-place, dislocated, deranged, "a long way from home." How else are we to learn such fundamental knowledge as comes from skin to skin, cheek to breast, except in her body, in her arms?

Perhaps it is that slow but inexorable movement outward from the womb of her body, the womb of her home, that we have such a hard time forgiving our mothers for. We say we rebel against the possessive mother, the one who tries to tie us to her apron strings. But the cry of the angry adolescent is, "I didn't ask to be born!" We didn't ask to be launched into the world, singular and solitary. Indeed, it is beyond our capacity to desire such a destiny. What we ask is to remain in the comfort of the ignorant darkness, to continue in the delusion that we are the universe. And however gently and gradually we are weaned from that illusion —and that task is almost exclusively a mother's—we still harbor a certain resentment at our plight. Not only are we not the whole universe, but the rest of the world seems increasingly oblivious to our necessity as we grow older. From family to school to work-a-day world, we are thrust ever outward down an apparently endless birth canal contracted with unbearable pressure. No wonder the metaphor of being born again is not a particularly popular one.

"A peculiar chemistry takes place at the door of my parents' house," Laurel Lee recounts. "Somehow, between turning the simulated brass doorknob and stepping onto the beige carpet, my molecules lose their structure. I stand in need of reconstruction." She is crying out, as all of us do sooner or later, against the inadequacy of that first birth. The accouterments of our parents' lives cannot possibly express the truth of our own. The wonder is that we should ever expect them to.

Some people would have us dismantle the whole structure

of the self in order to move it off its flawed foundation. There are cracks, sometimes gaping holes, in that early knowledge of the world supplied by our mothers—all manner of things she never told us about. Or perhaps her own information was faulty or inadequate. How shall we ever build ourselves more stately mansions until we can clear away the rubble of that flawed foundation we have had to depend on since childhood?

But life, I think, is too short for that. Rebuilding a whole self from scratch is a perilous undertaking. And what psychic contractor will presume to guarantee the finished product, or even the stability of the new footing? That foundational encounter with the world can come at only one point in our life, our mortal life. If our introduction into this world has been limited and inadequate through some maternal failing, well, best to shore ourselves up at the weak points than cut ourselves loose from the only mooring we have in this dangerous world. All of us are limited to one history, one time and place of birth. Each of us opened his eyes and ears on a particular day for the first time. We cannot roam the world like dissatisfied spirits seeking to insert themselves into now one body, now another. We are limited to one history. And that might be more of a blessing than we sometimes realize.

In fairy tales we can see this desire to dispose of our unsatisfactory origins. It happens this way in such stories. All the good mothers die off early, at just about the time the child-hero is at an age to find them inadequate. They are replaced, if at all, by wicked stepmothers. Thus the memory of the mother is safely venerated. She's not around to muddy the waters for her offspring any more. But the fairy tale stepmother, that surrogate, that impostor, can be exposed as a failure because she has no true, direct connection with the child. Snow White's wicked stepmother was a veritable witch. She gazed into her magic mirror and discovered that she was no longer the fairest in the land.

There comes a point for all of us, I suppose, when the flaws in our parents are revealed. The ideal is appraised and found wanting. Even the mother who has honestly tried to convince her child of her human fallibility will have that honesty taken for humility—until one sad day when her child is startled by the truth.

When we ask the mythic mirror on the wall to reveal the fairest one of all, somehow it always turns out to be us. We are the standard by which our mothers are judged, at least in that arbitrary age of adolescence. But as we grow older and more reflective ourselves, the image in the mirror wavers. I look at my mother now to discover myself mirrored in her. It is uncanny how clear the picture is. No longer do I perceive only her failings in her; I perceive *my* failings in her. What I early took to be the pattern of perfection, this shining surface crazed with rifts and fissures, this cracked idol is—myself. No one else could, I know, point out to me with such profit my flaws. I learned my first life lessons from her. I am her reflection; now she mirrors me. And I take heed, take warning. What more could one human being do for another?

I say I want my daughters to fulfill their destinies. Where did I get such a high-flown ideal? From my mother, who wanted the same for me. But this was not the mindless absorption of an ingested notion. This heritage received at the hands of my mother, this belief in a destiny to be fulfilled, has to be tested in the hottest fires this world can provide.

There is a woman in Eliot's poem, *The Wasteland,* who frantically inquires, "What shall I do now? What shall I ever do? ... What shall we do to-morrow? What shall we ever do?" That is the eternal cry of those who get up in the morning to no destiny, and it has been mine on many an empty, pointless Sunday afternoon. One watches the light drain out of the sky, then turns to the other in the room with the question, "What shall we do now?" While no doubt my mother, unbeknownst to me, blew prayers into my pitifully shrunken little destiny to keep it alive. And slowly, painfully, that ideal passed through conflagrations where false fancies and seeming dreams go up in smoke. Hankerings, itches, short-circuited sputterings of a will that is only self-propelled— these all at last fall away and are licked up by tongues of flame whose appetite is inconsolable.

As a child, one wants grand things: palaces, kingdoms, flight. Adults settle for a promotion, a house with an extra bathroom, the chair of a committee, an affair with an insurance salesman. All because they have ceased to believe in anything so grand as a destiny, a thing more eternal than stars, more final than death. But a mother retains those great expectations, even when her child has renounced them.

Poor Monica, mother of Saint Augustine, object of ridicule by contemporary church historians and, no doubt, a comic figure in many ways, wept and prayed continually for her brilliant, arrogant son's conversion. She went to her bishop, a path often beaten by well-meaning mothers, to plead with this sagacious priest to have a talk with the headstrong young man and convince him of the error of his ways. I can hear her arguments now. "You're an educated man. He'll listen to you. He thinks I'm just a foolish old woman." The priest wisely refused, divining that Augustine was as yet "unripe for instruction" because he was still "brimming over with the novelty of the heresy." But Monica persisted with her entreaties. And the bishop, finally losing his patience like the unjust judge of the parable, tells her to be off and leave him in peace, yet gives her this consolation that she took as a heavenly message: "It cannot be that the son of these tears should be lost."

The tears of Monica, the importunate widow. Without them, what impoverishment the world would have suffered. Is it the dogged determination of such women, bereft of dignity and hanging on with bared teeth, that preserves our destinies for us, that snatches them from the flames? There was only one person who would have taken Christ's place on the cross. The one to whom Simeon prophesied, "And a sword will pierce through your own soul also."

I remember word for word my own mother broaching before my baptism the subject of my soul's salvation. In the middle of some chore or other she spoke, made awkward by her earnestness. "It's the most important decision you'll ever make," she said, gouging out the eye of a potato. "More important even than getting married."

Well, *of course!* I wanted to exclaim, my eight-year-old indignation all but overcoming me. Just about *anything* was more important than getting married. Who cares about that! Her remark had the opposite effect of her intention, though I doubt she ever knew it. It seemed to me that she was demeaning my precious destiny by comparing it to something as mundane as marriage.

And off I went down a rabbit hole into my own secret thoughts, oblivious to the weighty point she was trying to make.

But I still remember—word for word.

I knew, for years had known because I was taught it unconsciously every day, that I was a creature of destiny, of solemn significance, urgent to the universe. No wonder the world of getting and spending for cheap pleasure and expensive pain tasted like sawdust later on. My appetite for fantastic fortunes had been whetted by the pearl of great price my mother dangled before me.

"Do whatever he tells you," Mary said to the servants at the Cana wedding. Mary, Monica, my mother all shared this serene confidence in their offspring. It was part of the given of my existence that whatever noble quest I set out upon could not fail but come to pass. I was not left awash in a sea of doubt and indecision as to my abilities—nor my responsibilities for them. I knew who I was because my mother told me. And who should know better than she who, in conspiracy with God, had concocted me in her own body?

I have no reason to doubt all the tales told today by women about their childhoods, bent and truncated by the impoverished roles they were forced into. But this was never part of my experience. Never once was I warned away from any feat, either physical or intellectual, because of my sex. Indeed, how could destiny's darling be subject to such a quibbling consideration? Is my experience really all that unusual?

And my knowledge of who I was—who *we* were—did not all come from talk. My mother washed, ironed, cooked, sewed, always with competence and sometimes artistry. She also milked cows, grew flowers and vegetables, picked wild berries in deep, thorny thickets, killed copperheads with a hoe, wrung the necks of chickens with a grim and fine flourish, and went off wearing make-up to work in large, mysterious buildings where people wore their dress-up clothes. She attacked a typewriter as she did the chickens—no funny business. To see the words come out, dark and perfect on the white sheet, was miracle and ecstasy to me.

Nancy Friday begins her book *My Mother, My Self* with this accusation: "I have always lied to my mother. And she to me." The only lie I think my mother ever told me concerned a baby chick, dyed green, I got for Easter when I was five. It disappeared one morning and she told me it had run away. So implicit was my trust in her truthfulness that I could picture it, gleeful and free, sprinting down the driveway to seek its fortune.

But my mother would have "soon as lied to me" about any matter of consequence as sold me into slavery. She apprised me of some very unpleasant facts from time to time. She informed me in no uncertain terms when something was none of my business. She teased and joked. But she did not lie. To this day I'm not sure but what the baby chick didn't run away.

I can still remember the sternness with which my mother called me to her to confront some misdeed. "I'd rather see you lying here dead before me than to know you'd told me a lie." Her long finger would point to the hypothetical coffin at her feet, and I would grow dizzy with guilt, tasting the offending words like alum on my tongue.

Perhaps she overdid it, this hatred of deception. Perhaps it accounts for the skeptical air with which I now approach the world. But it gave me an unshakable respect for the word, one's word, a thing not to be broken on any account. The truth embodied in words. And an imperishable contempt for words used to deceive or simply used shabbily.

Inevitably, of course, I discovered the gulf between my family's private estimation of me and society's devaluing indifference. Raised to believe in special purposes and high callings, I confronted a world where the best that was offered was a score on an aptitude test. And how would I have held out, solitary in my bunker of selfhood, without certain visions of my mother herself as a creature transcending the commonplace, an immortal in disguise?

There was an ice storm once when we lived on the farm. Encased in a thick glazing of ice, the trees glistened and clicked together. Out in the woods and along the road we could hear the branches clashing and tinkling as the wind blew through them. At times whole trees collapsed under the weight of the ice in loud, crashing clamor. There was danger and destruction in the storm; power lines fell and roads were blocked. But we were also besieged by beauty. Myriad sparkling reflections, light caught in the intricate tracery of lifted and arcing limbs, parabolas of clattering ice. It was the world of the Snow Queen, both beautiful and perilous.

My brother and I went out at night and down our lane to the gate. The moon shone near the full on a crystal world. In the night's blue shadows the moonlight glanced off the trees as their limbs tinkled trembling together. Into this magic scene suddenly rode our mother on the back of our white mare which we most often saw hitched to the wagon. But tonight the mare was as magic as our mother who sat high above us now on the horse, looking down like the Snow Queen herself, amused at our surprise. A woman on a white horse caught in a crystal net of ice and moonlight. After a moment she laughed and rode on. My mother and more. She had her own secret self with her that night on the back of the white horse. And it frightened me.

The mystery, hallowed and awful, of a separate self broke in upon me. The woman on horseback amid the ice and moonlight was more than my mother. She had an existence apart from me. She was a creature from another world, one I knew little about. She inhabited a place where I could not go. I only had a glimpse of that startling truth then. Now I have learned to live with it as a familiar fact. She did not live just to be the receptacle of my own marvelous creation. She, too, has a self that stands solitary and inviolate before God. She has a face.

Mother, we name this woman who brought us into being. A universal name, a symbolic title. Then one day we discover, if we can bear the sight, the singularity of that hooded figurine. She has her own name. And we are frightened and even angry.

We transfer a good deal of our understanding of our mothers to our understanding of God. Or, as one of the daughters in Evelyn Waugh's novel, *Brideshead Revisited,* says, "I sometimes think when people wanted to hate God they hated Mummy."

There is more to that metaphor of being born again, born of the Spirit, than we have admitted. When Jesus used that description of our destiny, it was not a lucky stroke of invention or a mere figure of speech. It means, quite literally, that God is our Mother as surely as our Father. The Spirit bears us, gives birth to us, nurtures us. We are upheld, weightless, within those amniotic waves "in the Spirit."

God is a name like *Mother,* universal and generic. A name we are startled into calling out involuntarily in the dark. And sometimes I think this is what we want God to be: the Mother without a face. Ever accessible, always protecting, but blank and featureless. The children of Israel pleaded with Moses that they would not have to meet Yahweh face to face at Sinai: "Let not God speak with us lest we die."

We are shaken to our roots when we discover that God has purposes beyond our own. We are angered when this hooded, faceless provider turns out to be more than a convenience to sustain our lives. We are terrified when he thrusts us out of ourselves, makes demands, insists on our being more than we were even capable of desiring. No wonder we resent him and rebel. No one ever took it into his head to kill God until he acquired a human face.

Augustine asks his readers to pray for his mother and father: "With pious hearts let them remember those who were not only my parents in this light that fails, but were also my brother and sister. . . ."

This woman who sits on the side of my bed smoothing the sheets with her hand—I am just beginning to see her face, to learn her name, this sister of mine, this daughter of God.

CHAPTER SIX

Black Sheep

I have saints in my family. They know how to suffer
fools gladly. Sometimes they even know the fools they
suffer to be themselves.

But for every saint in this family, there are at least a dozen
sad apostates. The few saints' lives are like scattered green shoots
poking through the rubble left by the collapsed edifice of family.

For what we meant by family a generation ago is now a
deserted definition. We drive through the countryside where I
grew up and see gray ghosts of homesteads, old frame farmhouses
the weather has scoured sitting in the middle of emerald alfalfa
fields. They once held as many as three or four generations to-

gether. Now they are stuffed with hay. It straggles out the windows like the wadding in a discarded doll's head. Once human habitations, the houses seem somehow desecrated by their use as makeshift barns. They lean in the direction of the prevailing winds, an outward and visible sign of a deserted sacrament.

When I was a little girl, the high point of our summer was the Fourth of July family reunion. It somewhat resembled the Jewish Feast of Booths in that the overnight guests stayed in whatever accommodations they could devise. We converged on the homestead of the oldest living relative, over a hundred strong. I have no idea what a horror it must have been to the hostess. Children never consider such things. I do remember that the plumbing, never too sturdy during the best of times, was inevitably overloaded.

But for children it was better than birthdays. There were cousins you hadn't seen all year to eye suspiciously and measure yourself against, clots of gossipers to eavesdrop on, dares given and taken to catch the pony or swim in the muddy stock tank. The food was the product of a tacit cooking contest between the kitchens of cousins. Your own parents could never find you, and your aunts and uncles permitted almost anything. You could run under the big live oaks till you sagged with the damp heat, eat whatever came to hand, sleep where you dropped. And all the while you were surrounded by a gallery of grown-ups from which to pick and choose a pattern for fantasy. Constantly weighing and evaluating, my child's mind considered who I most wanted to be like. Here one could, at close range, weigh good humor with good looks, sobriety against elevated spirits, braggadocio with reticence. Even for the grown-ups, I think it was like getting measured every year against the doorpost. Each brought his own standard with him, held it up to the others, certainly, and perhaps more furtively, to himself.

The reunions now are much more attenuated affairs. They're not held at old homesteads any more, but at a rented park pavilion with air conditioning and playground equipment. No one can stand the heat any more. No one stays overnight. The plumbing is never taxed.

I haven't been to one myself in over a decade. Consequently I have little idea of what's happening in the lives of most of my cousins, many of whom I haven't seen since I stopped going to the reunions. The only time I'm likely to see them now is at funerals. My reunions these days are with individuals. I sometimes see an aunt, singly. I always visit the great-aunts and grandparents. I still use them for measuring sticks, just as one stands next to the mastodon bones in the museum to judge how large the world used to be. But I never encounter that entire constellation, made up of myriad satellites, that we used to mean by family.

I do collect a certain amount of data about my cousins from my mother though. They all live a life of considerably more ease and convenience than their parents or grandparents did. They have, by and large, come up in the world, although the world in general has come up along with them. The divorce rate among them is perhaps slightly higher than the national average as is the alcoholism, but neither is any worse than their parents' generation, surprisingly enough. There is some small sour comfort to be derived, I suppose, from knowing the disintegration did not begin with us.

To my knowledge there was only one drug addict in my crop of progeny, and he was killed in a shoot-out in the city several years ago at an age that ought to have been tender. I remember him as a muscular little baby my aunt, to the horror of the older generation, used to toast to a medium brown by naked sunbaths.

Just about all my cousins live a good deal closer to home than I do. Many of them are more stable than their parents, although they are just now coming into their own with the discovery of mid-life crisis.

I take this kind of inventory because I wonder at times why there are no more real reunions, why we have so little to say to one another now. As children, my cousins and I all agreed on the value of ghost stories, of hide-and-seek, horses, and chocolate pie. Although I imagine that today our children would be just as fascinated with one another and just as unified in their desires, for us as adults the fierceness of those summer days, thirty years later, has been damped to only a tepid curiosity—who's living where, has what job, how many marriages, divorces, diseases, children. All the bonds that tie the heart are attached elsewhere now, and the question of desire has been buried or lost.

My mother had eight siblings; I have one. During the Depression of the 1930s and World War II she lived with enclaves of aunts and uncles and cousins. During Vietnam and Watergate I lived on a commune with transient friends. In one generation the apostasy from family has been accomplished. Why do we, who used to hold hands and huddle together in hiding places, all look at one another so blankly now?

I spend an afternoon with one of those relatives who used to be my companion at the reunions. We were girls together, as close as sisters, at times living in the same house, catching the same school bus. She's filing for her third divorce. She has a psychiatrist. Her doctor says the tests show she has no self-esteem. I don't know what's happened to it, under what circumstances it has evaporated, because she always had plenty as a child. She was always more daring than I was. I lived in terror of the malicious black rooster that waited in ambush under their front porch, but not her. She would rush at it, shrieking and flailing her arms until, bluffed, it would stalk away. She would even straddle the calves in the barn and ride them, pitching and squealing, around the pen. Against her shining dark braids and eager brown eyes, I always showed up mousy and sulky.

Her mother, a fierce old woman who died last year, had her periods of instability too. She had visions and heard voices. She would pace the dark house at night, pleading for forgiveness for her sins, which though real enough and even mundane, acquired a certain extravagance from her manner of repentance. She kept her radio tuned to stations broadcasting bizarre doctrines and appeals for donations from Mexico where the power and frequency were unregulated. Everyone put her problems down to isolation and a bad conscience. She lived in a backwoods farmhouse at the time and had little enough contact with the outside world. And sure enough, over the years and after a move to town, her temper gradually improved and she gained a certain cheerful serenity. Her religion modulated to a private recipe made up of *World Tomorrow* broadcasts and certain primitive Baptist sects.

I don't know how she would have scored on a test for self-esteem. That category, like computers, had not been invented in her day. She would not have known what such mental health terminology signified. But somehow her instabilities were at least more picturesque than her daughter's, which smack sadly of soap operas.

During my childhood, this woman was a fearful and unknown quantity, not to be crossed on any account. I did not think of her as representative of a category of emotional maladjustment. On the contrary, she was unique. Whatever was wrong with her could not be labeled. She couldn't buy a book at the checkout stand of the supermarket to find herself defined. She had to make it up as she went along.

The daughter left behind those ghostly airwaves that haunted the farmhouse in the evening and took up the northern faith of her husband's family. If we want to make correlations here, we can say that the daughter's religious affiliation, like her emotional disruptions, has become mainline.

Apostasy, it seems, like divorce, is a family affair. Leaving a faith and leaving a family go together. In fact, it is probably more often the family that is being rejected than the faith. The simulated brass doorknobs and the beige carpet rather than any actual dogma. The predictable Sunday menus, the set holiday rituals, the peculiar figures of speech rather than the tenets of faith.

How could one possibly apostatize without a family? It may be difficult for me to imagine acquiring a faith without a family to inherit it from since that has not been my experience. However, I know that this does happen. In fact, it happened that way to my husband, whose own conversion coincided with that of his parents and whose family life, up to that point, was somewhat chaotic in comparison to the measured, predictable forms of my own. But to leave a faith, to reject it, renounce it, one must first have a family that embodies it. You can find faith without a family, but you can't lose it without one.

My childhood companion defected from the faith of her mother, but not because of any rational reevaluation of its doctrine, if indeed she ever had a clear notion of what that doctrine was. What she left were the skirts that always had to be two inches longer than her classmates'; the shaped-note songbooks; the proud self-exclusion from the parties, the clothes, and the cosmetics of her friends. And most of all the poverty that such sects seem to succor.

If she never considered her denominational shift a defection, certainly her mother did. And if in later years her own good nature overcame the disapproval her sect obliged her to feel toward her daughter, she nevertheless would have credited the rents in the family's social fabric to the laxness fostered by modern churches.

Calculating the rate of apostasy is a more delicate task than calculating the divorce rate. There are records of baptisms, but like vaccinations, some don't "take." And the cross-pollination of denominations has spread like an epidemic throughout what used to be a one-church family. Also, unless one drops dead from it, like Ananias and Sapphira, apostasy is sometimes difficult to detect.

Yet pious families are not immune. Indeed, at times apostasy seems to break out in a particularly virulent strain among priestly families. Eli, the priest at Shiloh, had two sons, Hophni and Phineas, who made a practice of extorting from the people the sacrifices slaughtered for the altar and of seducing the women who served at the tabernacle. Although they lived with the very ark of the covenant, it could not protect them from their own reprobation.

Actually the ark seems to have been able to exert more power over foreign gods than over backsliding Israelites, for when the Philistines carried it into their temple to add it to their deity collection, the idol Dagon is reported to have fallen flat on its face before the ark.

Since Eli's sons had proved unsatisfactory to succeed him, the Lord had to raise up a priest for himself from another family altogether, and Samuel was chosen. But as it happened, Samuel's own sons eventually proved to be no more a credit to their father than Eli's sons had. Joel and Abijah managed to get priestly posts at Beersheba, but so flagrant was their corruption that the elders came to Samuel and begged him to restructure the entire legal system so that they might have a king to replace these unjust local magistrates. Thus, the greatest priests of Israel were unable to foster faith and fear of the Lord within their own households.

But let us not consign that kind of apostasy, that severe reversal the faith can suffer from one generation to the next, to the age of the Old Testament. Only a few miles from my parents' home, in fact in the same county, Trinity, where my elder kinswoman wrestled with her visions, the infamous Texas outlaw John Wesley Hardin grew up in the latter half of the nineteenth century. As his name might suggest, Hardin was the son of a Methodist minister. Yet he committed his first murder at the early age of fifteen, and continued to notch his gun until, by his eighteenth birthday, he had killed twenty-three men, some for no more than an unfriendly remark made on the street or for jostling his pride in public.

Yet for all his violent nature, he was never deserted by his family. His father seems to have frowned more on his predilection for gambling than for murder. In fact his parents frequently moved their residence in order to be closer to their maverick son. He, in turn, visited his family frequently, even when such reunions had to be surreptitious. And in the end, the only way the Texas Rangers had of handling him was through secret messages sent by go-betweens threatening to hold members of his family responsible for his actions. Hardin took the threats seriously because a mob had already lynched his older brother, Joe, whose good name and position as a county official had not been sufficient to protect him from their outrage.

If John Wesley Hardin, the Methodist minister's son, remains one of Texas's most notorious men of violence, it is not because the breed has died out. One of the stories I hear on this trip concerns my great-aunt's pastor, whose son could rival Absalom for the shame and sorrow he has brought on his family. In fact, John Wesley Hardin's apostasy was amazingly ambiguous. He never really renounced either his family or his faith, although he brought disgrace to both. And later in prison he became the Sunday school superintendent. But his contemporary counterpart leaves no doubts in the mind; he has apostatized with a vengeance.

The way my great-aunt tells the story, it all started with an automobile—the same way the Fall, in the popular mind, began with an apple. From the moment this boy began driving the car his daddy unwisely gave him, he "went to the bad," as she puts it, drinking and carousing, stealing guns and saddles, vandalizing property. Even as a youngster he was guilty of a good deal of gratuitous violence and a generally unsavory character. Eventually there was a shotgun wedding with another preacher's daughter, but married life didn't seem to settle him down any.

In fact, he got involved with yet another daughter of the clergy, this time in the city about seventy miles away. When he discovered that she was pregnant, he shot her, came back home, and had his wife empty out the contents of her cedar chest. Then at gun point, as the trial testimony goes, he forced her to accompany him back to the city where together they stuffed the body, doubled over, into the chest. They carried the chest and its contents back out to the country and buried it in a shallow grave in an old abandoned cemetery just east of my great-aunt's place.

The crime was eventually discovered, although there is a difference of opinion as to just how. My great-aunt says the young man confessed under questioning. My cousin contends he was overheard bragging about the crime in a bar. Others remember that the heavy rains that spring washed the soft earth from around the chest, exposing the grave. The papers reported that the victim kept a diary incriminating the young man.

He was paroled once, but after shooting a man in a brawl, was soon back at the prison farm, not far from where his family lives. Since then he has escaped once. It was on a summer Sunday evening. At dusk the state troopers surrounded the little country church where his father was preaching, their floodlights illuminating the building like a stage set. The father came out and begged them to pull back from the church so that the worshipers would not be disturbed. At this point in the story, my great-aunt pauses to remark in amazement, "And Brother Darrell had to go right ahead and bring the message, knowing his child was out there somewhere being hunted down."

Happily, however, when the son got to the river, he saw the police sitting out in a boat waiting for him and heard the trackers coming up behind him in the woods with the dogs. He surrendered quietly that time.

He has, however, repeatedly threatened to escape and kill his wife who, as my aunt says, "stuck with him through it all," and their three children who are "the best beloved youngsters you'd ever want to see."

Meanwhile, Brother Darrell preaches on, his ministry

seemingly as unimpaired by the misdeeds of his offspring as Samuel's was by those of his sons.

Such stories are enough to convince one of the value of a celibate clergy. Hophni and Phineas, Joel and Abijah, John Wesley Hardin, Brother Darrell's son. Perhaps they all suffered from an immune reaction to the faith of their fathers. Perhaps some form of apostasy is necessary to every generation. Perhaps we instinctively feel the need to transcend the birth of the flesh, even when we abort the birth of the spirit. Perhaps these disastrous attempts to break free of the fleshly father took their rise from an ill-formed desire for a spiritual one. For didn't those recorded as spiritual successes also have to first break with their earthly fathers?

Didn't Abraham himself leave his father's household and set out for an unknown land? Surely that was viewed as betrayal, defection, treason to the family. Didn't Joseph, the father's favorite, have to be forced out of the nest by his jealous brothers who turned out to be his unwitting benefactors? Is it not the prodigal who is reconciled to the father at the end of the parable and not his elder brother who made a point of never leaving home? Was not Jesus himself considered an apostate in his own day? Wasn't his very physical dislocation, his wandering from Galilee to Judea, the visible sign of his freedom from family ties? John Wesley Hardin may have hid out in half the towns in Texas trying to escape his pursuers, but at least he kept in touch with his family. Jesus traveled about from town to village, seemingly without thought for those he left behind at home. By neglecting his duties to his family as the eldest son, he was himself a prodigal. No wonder he was seen through the eyes of the law-abiding citizens of his day as the leader of a band of desperadoes, men whom he also lured from their family obligations. And in the end he, too, died the death of an outlaw who had put himself above the bonds and constraints of society.

It was in the house of a stranger that Jesus, the apostate Jew, renounced his very mother and brothers who had come—as all loyal, decent relations would—to take the unfortunate madman home, as John Wesley Hardin's family continually pleaded with him to come home and settle down. Jesus turned his back on not only his religion but on his family, in a way the gunslinger never did. And in their places he put the strangers seated around him.

Whether or not apostasy is an essential element in the salvation of all covenant children, the example of Jesus encourages me. Maybe my own defections have been more than just a detour—have even been essential to my destiny. Perhaps every generation faces the obligation to renew its vows to the Lord.

CHAPTER SEVEN

Earthen Vessels

On 18 June 1921, Evelyn Waugh wrote in his diary: "In the last few weeks I have ceased to be a Christian. I have realized that for the last two terms at least I have been an atheist in all except the courage to admit it to myself." Waugh found that there was nothing particularly unusual in his situation. Many of his classmates were undergoing the same transformation. With his characteristic asperity he remarks, "I suffered no sense of loss in discarding the creed of my upbringing; still less of exhilaration."

A gentler soul, but one of no less rigorous veracity, George MacDonald, wrote to his father as a young student: "All my

77

teaching in youth seems useless to me. I must get it all from the Bible again."

Waugh ended up an adult convert to the Roman Catholic church. MacDonald, forced to resign from the pastorate of the Congregational Church of Arundel, Scotland, became a writer whose works are now a treasure of the church. For many, apostasy is a pupal state: a nonfeeding, often immobile transformation stage between the larva and the imago states. These sleepers emerge from their confinement resplendent after a long night of doubt and denial.

But the destiny of an insect is more certain than that of a human being. The movement of apostasy is not always onward and upward. The chronicles of the kings of Israel and Judah show more reversions to paganism than conversions to the one true God.

Beginning with Solomon, David's son, there was a steady decline in the orthodoxy of the nation's leadership. Solomon looked with a tolerant eye on the variegated deities of his cosmopolitan wives. His son Rehoboam, a weak tyrant who surrounded himself with sycophants, succeeded first in losing the northern half of the kingdom to a military junta headed by Jeroboam and then opening what was left of it to every religious franchise in the region.

The old gods returned with a vengeance. They had reigned in Canaan for centuries before this upstart deity, who called himself with incredible presumption "I-am," appeared.

The old gods extracted a terrible price for their protection. Perhaps that is why they were so irresistible; they allowed their worshipers to think they got what they paid for. At any rate, the defection from Yahweh to the local cults cost the children of Abraham, Isaac, and Jacob dearly. Their apostasy was no mere matter of switching denominations, or a difference in hymn tunes or sacramental styles. It was a descent into blood and barbarity, a desecration of the community and violation of the individual personality.

Ahab, the king of Israel notorious for his worship of Canaanite gods, reinstituted the old custom of immolating his children at the foundation of a new city. Later his counterpart in Judah, Ahaz, began the same practice. Ritual prostitution carried on to insure the fertility of the land shared the same quarters as the worship of Yahweh. The obliteration of the person in order to act out the demands of the deity was not an interesting philosophical speculation but a daily reality. The very definition of what it meant to be a human being hung in the balance.

In the northern kingdom of Israel, the corruption of both religious and civil life was unrelieved. And interestingly enough, the change from one dynastic line to another occurred there with dizzying regularity, while in the southern kingdom, Judah, the Davidic line was maintained until the Exile. Even the mothers of the kings of Judah are recorded. But in Israel the constant coups made not only the tracing of inheritance somewhat more tenuous but also the effect of fathers upon sons a moot point.

While all the kings of Israel are condemned by the compilers of their history as apostates, in Judah there were at least a handful who earned the historians' praise: Asa, Jehosaphat, Hezekiah, and Josiah. The rest were either half-hearted in their religious reforms or thoroughgoing in their apostasy.

It takes us by surprise to learn from the biblical record that the Passover was never celebrated in Jerusalem by the kings of Israel or Judah (not even by David) until the time of Josiah, one of the last kings in Judah's twilight years when it was already a vassal state. Indeed, the religious life of the Israelites was not one of orderly orthodoxy until after their return from exile. From the time when they were made a people in the desert and throughout the rule of the judges and the kings, Yahweh was jostled on every side by competitors. The Israelites never saw anything wrong with hedging their bets. They kept up their worship of this unique desert deity, but they also kept a corner for Moloch and Astarte. Inside the very temple at Jerusalem were shrines to astrological deities and accommodations for the male shrine prostitutes. And the priests of Yahweh belonged to professional organizations made up of pagan priests from the pluralistic society they lived in. Prosperity, in fact, seemed inevitably linked to apostasy. Only their later adversity brought forth the kind of strict orthodoxy that flourished among the Pharisees of Jesus' day.

My own apostasy as a child began with a preference for sliced bread. For generations my family had been eating buttermilk biscuits and cornbread made fresh each day. Such bread was not only the staple of their diet but their ritual of unity. It expressed their shared identity more deeply and thoroughly than any doctrinal statement. Like any efficacious communion bread, it was deeper than words and pervaded their being, defining them unconsciously.

Sliced bread and I were both products of World War II. During that demanding era women came out of the kitchen and into the wage-labor force. Bread, like everything else, began to be made in production lines. But what my family reluctantly accepted as a symbol of disruption and dislocation, I embraced as the real stuff, the way things were. When the war was over, I continued to choose what my family still calls "light bread" over the biscuits heavy with shortening or the crumbling cornbread. It became a symbol of my protest in the household and the subject of many affronted remarks. Even the pagan priests in Judah, left unemployed by Josiah's reforms, came to Jerusalem, we're told, and ate the same unleavened bread as their fellow professionals. But I did not maintain even that link. I broke faith first with my family's food. They felt the offense, sensing it would somehow lead to further unorthodoxies down the road. And it did.

I still remember when I came across Shelley's essay, "The Necessity of Atheism," in high school. I responded no doubt to its aesthetic value even more than to its logic, but the document presented my sixteen-year-old mind with a rationalization for a rebellion I had already begun to make against the bread and faith of my fathers. Shelley's words were like gunpowder thrown on coals. Feverishly I read portions to my mother, who only shook her head and went on with her work. She didn't argue. She didn't even see what all the fuss was about.

There are times when two people can only stare at one another across the twenty years that separate them. I'm sure I knew, even before I began, that my mother's faith was unshakable. I had seen every evidence of that throughout my young life. But I had never heard her argue any point of dogma, only affirm her faith. And there was no way to tell a sixteen-year-old, just discovering analytical thinking, that one proves the truth of life finally by living it, not by slicing it up into syllogisms; that God, being a person, is not made up of propositions.

No doubt she did the right thing by refusing to be drawn, though at the time I was infuriated at her easy dismissal of what was to me a dire dilemma. If she had argued, I would have been forced into the fortress of my own mind. And we would have both ended in falsifying our true positions through the need to throw up defensive barricades around ourselves. As it was, I was left to wander about like a free lance, tilting at whatever windmills came my way.

Nothing could have pleased me more. I was eager to set out, like the fairy-tale hero, to seek my spiritual fortune. When the prodigal son left home, he went to a far country where he wasted his substance on riotous living. Somewhat more fastidious, or perhaps only more timorous, I went away to college to study literature and philosophy. But I did manage to put eight hundred significant miles between my family and me.

Indeed, geographical shift often seems the necessary concomitant to apostasy. Leaving home has to be literal. For one thing, I was certain that only people who ate light bread could understand Shelley. I used to watch the little green lizards that live at the roots of houses in Texas and crawl out to sit in the sun during the day; I knew that I too would soon turn into one of those lizards, my brain reduced to its reptilian stump, if I didn't get out of there and into the far country. The languorous, easy air I breathed at home impeded achievement. Analytical thinking demanded a more astringent atmosphere.

Whatever my arrogance then, I don't think I was totally misguided in my intuitions. I have observed that topology and weather do indeed seem to make their own contributions to the shapes faith takes, just as they dictate the kinds of vegetation the land will sustain. Northern latitudes produce an austerity of both thought and feeling. Abstractions come easier in the crystallized air of Michigan than in Louisiana where life is languid and liquid, flowing into leisured narratives. Wyoming produces a certain proud self-protectiveness that comes from wrestling with emptiness and isolation. Mystics seem drawn to the desert. Even Jesus went to the wilderness to fast and pray.

So, like Abraham, I left my father's household behind and set out, not knowing where I was to go. If faith was not my motivation, it still made possible my setting out—the faith that had been the amniotic fluid in which I had floated so effortlessly all my life. I had fed on my family's faith as a germinating sprout feeds on the stored starches in the seed. And because I had grown up in a wealth of faith, I had the capital to begin my own search. It takes the hoarded strength of faith, put down in the roots' repository underground, to supply the potency to doubt, to search, even to frame the questions. This is the inheritance the prodigal takes with him.

James Baldwin in *Notes of a Native Son* looks back at his own apostasy from the faith of his father, a preacher in Harlem and, according to his son's description, the most bitter man he ever met. At fourteen Baldwin was himself a prodigy preacher at the Fireside Pentecostal Church in Harlem. Over the next three years he branched out to neighborhood storefront churches, drawing bigger crowds than his father, to James's vast satisfaction.

One of his father's favorite texts was Joshua 24:15, one I also frequently heard expounded as I was growing up: "And if it seem evil unto you to serve the Lord, choose you this day whom ye will serve; whether the gods which your fathers served that were on the other side of the flood, or the gods of the Amorites, in whose land ye dwell: but as for me and my house, we will serve the Lord." The sermons the father preached from that text were most often exhortations to cling to the family's faith, to salvage the household gods. But what the incipient apostate saw there was the repudiation of the gods the fathers had served. "With me and my house begins a new worship, a break with the traditions of the past." This was the way the young Baldwin, the up-and-coming teenage preacher, appropriated the scripture. The text became a weapon. He turned his father's own words against him—made them a repudiation of a man whose pain and cruelty he could not then understand nor forgive.

His father's funeral fell on Baldwin's nineteenth birthday. By that time the son had already given up preaching for writing and had made a fair amount of headway into the far country. The family drove the body to the graveyard through streets sown with shattered glass left from a race riot the day before. The ravaged streets seemed a portent of the very apocalypse that had inflamed his father to prophecy. "All my father's texts and song," Baldwin reflected, "which I had decided were meaningless, were arranged before me at his death like empty bottles, waiting to hold the meaning which life would give them for me."

We all apostatize in different ways. Not everyone takes up gunslinging and violence like John Wesley Hardin or the country preacher's son. Perhaps even fewer take the path of a greater fervor than their fathers, though there are instances of that too, even among the kings and prophets of Israel. Most, in a more genteel manner, simply shift denominations or become secularized.

But is apostasy necessary? Does, as William Blake and the parable of the prodigal claim, the road of excess lead to the palace of wisdom? Is it true, as C. S. Lewis wrote, that "Every idea of Him we form, He must in mercy shatter"? Can the "gods from the other side of the flood whom our fathers served" ever be carried across intact? Must God be newly born in each generation or else become no more than an idol that the great Iconoclast himself must destroy? Is all my forebears' experience of no use to me? Were all those Sunday school mornings, those drowsy, droning sermons, those Bible verses appended to the bottom of letters from home of no account?

John Updike, an apostate somewhat reticent about his mid-life reclamation, with that articulate lack of passion characteristic of the middle class of which he writes, credits his father, Wesley Updike, as the one who supplied the impetus for his return to the fold. "He was a great churchgoer, and I suppose that made it a more feasible thing for me to do," he told an interviewer. James Baldwin described the texts and songs of his father as empty bottles waiting to be filled with the meaning his own life would give them. "We have this treasure in earthen vessels," said Paul.

And earthen vessels, the shape of faith if not the content, are what apostates inherit from their fathers. There had to be some song, some scrap of text, for Baldwin to start from. Updike needed the memory of his father magnetized to a spiritual center in order to make a mandala of his own. No human being comes into the world fresh and original. We are all of us strung out across the long history of our race by those fine filaments of DNA. We are stitched to time and space with the twisted threads of chemically coded information. We are caught in that intricate and inescapable net of chromosomes. Even the way we fold our hands together, which thumb we put on top, is an inherited characteristic. Each of us is, at birth, already as old as the race.

There is, in nature, no new beginning. It is the same Adam who is born over and over. That is why the second birth, the gestation in and delivery by the Spirit, is absolutely essential. But the second birth does not negate the first, which is also the work of God and therefore good. We may transcend our chemical selves, but we may never cancel or deny the creation of which we are a part.

However much we may want to sever our ties to our ancestors, to cut ourselves loose from the failures and defects of inherited beliefs, our link to the patterns of the past are as inescapable as the imprint of our genes. Paul had to begin from his position as a Pharisee. Luther had to be an Augustinian monk before he could become a reformer. Even Jesus had to be a Jew, living within the framework of communal words and rituals, in order to be a part of the human experience. No one gets a clean, blank slate on which to scrawl his message to the world; it is already dusty with chalk and scribbled with markings from the past. But we all have to start somewhere. We all have to have an earthen vessel, inherited, common as clay, whose design we had no control over. We all have a place, particular and limited, our Haran, from which to set out.

It is time for me to leave again. The trip home, my annual interval as a child, has come to an end. It is time to turn west, where others are waiting for me. Still, the power of this place, home, is great. It lies here like the silent, potent core of a nuclear reactor, emitting energy from a hunk of primal matter.

In the early morning I say good-by to my grandfather, my oldest living kin. I have ridden to church in a wagon behind two slow-paced mules with this old man, the long leather reins threaded through his hard fingers. But the difference between our days lies in something besides the sociological fact that I ride to church in an automobile now. It lies in something more than the technology of air conditioning that has replaced the funeral-parlor fans we used to stir the sultry sermon air around our faces. It has to do with the very way the world smells now. And sounds. It has to do with loss. The slow creaking of the iron and wood of the wagon jarring over the dried mud ruts is gone. It has to do with time. Physically lived time. And distance, the thousand actual miles I have put between us. It has to do with the great, tall, shaggy pines rising out of the daybreak mist this morning as I leave. They come up silently over the hill, looming through the fog to see me off, the sad sentinels of a time left behind.

When I come down to earth again, it will be on the high desert floor. Dry, clear, featureless, innocent of sacred groves. With little to tie the heart to except the light itself.

CHAPTER EIGHT

The Crucible of Parenthood

The landscape of childhood is lush with images, with significant memories and visions that become emblems of one's destiny. Chesterton remembered the man with the key crossing the bridge, a cardboard character in a homemade stage set that to his child-mind embodied adventure, search, and gaiety. Cardinal Newman as a child thought himself an angel, disguised, among other secret seraphic agents. But it is also sadly true that, as Paul put it, when he became a man, he put away childish things.

All that thick growth of possibilities that surrounded us as children gets methodically hacked down by the cold steel machetes of maturity. We give up the foolish notions that we are changeling children stolen away from our true parents, themselves the glorious figures of myth. We surrender our ambitions to be pirates and princesses. In adolescence we still daydream in our secret gardens, but already the verdure of the imagination has been pruned and trained into social espaliers. Instead of Cinderella there is *Cherry Ames, Student Nurse*. The Hardy Boys move in to replace Jack the Giant-Killer.

By the time we leave high school there is only something called "career opportunities," a grave into which we dump all the dead dreams of childhood. "Welcome to the Real World," smirk the advisers.

The Real World is a desert, denuded of the lushness of childhood where anything was possible. Very little is possible in this adult aridity. Very little that a child finds interesting anyway. And growing up means settling for what you can get.

We must set out across this barren plain like refugees from the land of plenty. There's no going back. The road back is guarded by one of those very flaming figures of childhood possibility. Our own dreams turn against us. The eviction is irrevocable and inevitable.

Even Jesus, in order to get the full impact of what it is like to be human, had to pass through those gates. When Satan tempted him in the desert, it was with those last gleaming images of childhood: magic food, flight, kingdoms of splendor. But for him, as for any son of man, there was no going back, no retreat into the illusion of a childhood regained painlessly. It is not by a grasping regression that we lay hold of the treasures, but by submitting to a second birth.

Augustine, the African saint, described his dilemma at this austere entrance into adulthood.

> *I found much to bewilder me in my memories of the long time which had passed since I was nineteen, the age at which I had first begun to search in earnest for truth and wisdom and had promised myself that, once I had found them, I would give up all the vain hopes and mad delusions which sustained my futile ambitions. I realized that I was now thirty years old and was still floundering in the same*

quagmire, because I was greedy to enjoy what the world had to offer, though it only eluded me and wrested my strength. . . . I longed for a life of happiness but I was frightened to approach it in its own domain; and yet, while I fled for it, I still searched for it.

Now Augustine had fathered a child at about the same time that he began his search for truth and wisdom. The mother of the child was his mistress, a situation common enough among his class and contemporaries, although the fact that he continued to live with her for more than a decade after the birth of his son was perhaps not so common. Augustine's father had died the year before the child was born. In a sense, Augustine was hemmed in, trapped between those twin facts of death and birth. His father's death and his son's birth meant that his own implacable adulthood was upon him. He had no choice but to begin his search, one that lasted considerably longer than Christ's forty days in the desert, simply because Augustine found it impossible to say no to the temptations.

Nevertheless, through all those years of dissipation, the incipient saint did his duty by his child. In fact, Adeodatus ("God-given") grew up in the scholar-orator's household as his acknowledged son and must have received an extraordinary education there, since together the father and son devised a dialogue along classical lines *(De Magistro)* when the boy was only sixteen. "His intelligence left me spellbound," recorded the father whose own wit and mental prowess has astonished the centuries. Allowing for paternal pride, Adeodatus must indeed have been a marvel.

Augustine, even as a libertine, saw to it that his son was properly brought up, almost instinctively guarding his child's innocence from evil influences even as he himself went through the determined debauchery demanded by his times. Thus, after Augustine's conversion, both father and son were baptized and received into the church together. There must have been a certain comfort for the father's tender conscience in this, as he confessed in that book that must be the longest prayer ever recorded: "We made him our companion, in your grace no younger than ourselves. Together we were ready to begin our schooling in your ways. We were baptized, and all anxiety over the past melted away from us." There is not much more that we know about this child except that he died at the age of eighteen, the same age his father was when Adeodatus was born.

What effect did fatherhood have on this Carthaginian dilettante, this devotee of Mani, this dabbler in Platonism? Would his direction, his road toward his destiny have been the same without this child always there in the background, sitting in the shadows of the hearth? Was the boy a constraint on what otherwise might have been the life of a disengaged voluptuary, a fretful philosopher? Were his natural gifts, his grace and innocence, his spellbinding intelligence a constant if unwitting judgment on the father's life, a daily reminder of something not to be betrayed?

Is this the task our children perform for us? After we ourselves have passed through those gates and are on the far side of the flaming sword that guards them, do they act as reminders, letters from home, upon our memories and imaginations? Are they the catalyst that sparks our spiritual enterprise? In our concern for their destiny are we prodded to take stock of our own?

It was a child's voice Augustine heard calling in the garden at Milan, whether a boy or girl he said he could not tell. It was a singsong voice repeating the phrase, "Take it and read," as though in some child's game, that sent him to the Scripture. And for this very reason, it seemed to him the command of God. It was not the voice of wisdom or learning, nor of his intellectual friends who had been searching with him for metaphysical answers, nor of Ambrose the theologian, not even the imploring voice of Monica, his mother. Just the unconscious command of a child unaware of the part it was playing in a cosmic drama.

How great is our reliance on these little ones, even when we ourselves are as unaware of their influence on our lives as they are.

Eldridge Cleaver, another rebel, has said that the birth of his children was what began the reconsideration process for him. Just the fact of their coming into being was enough to bind him in a spell. And it was the desire to give their lives a shape that would recall his own, to surround them with the familiarities of his own childhood, that was the catalyst for his return from exile to his once-despised homeland. In the end, his son's opportunity to play football was a greater spiritual force than his own political plans for uniting the workers of the world.

Margaret Mead, the American anthropologist, having given up all hope of having children of her own, devoted her considerable energies to studying the children of other cultures. Then in the mid-1930s she found herself confronted with a tribe of cannibals in New Guinea that, despite her training in scientific detachment, aroused a profound horror in her. Infanticide was common among the Mundugumor. If a child proved to be the wrong sort to fortify a parent's tribal extra-sex rivalry (the mothers wanting sons and the fathers wanting daughters), either parent might toss the baby in the river, still living and wrapped in bark. Others might pull the floating container out, check to see what sex the child was, and throw it away again. "I reacted so strongly against the set of the culture," she wrote, "that it was here that I decided that I would have a child no matter how many miscarriages it meant. It seemed clear to me that a culture that so repudiated children could not be a good culture. . . . I saw for the first time what the active refusal of children could do to a society."

Children were the catalyst that, in Mead's interior alchemy, transmuted both the woman and her work. Thereafter she had a standard by which to measure human societies. And perhaps with less scientific basis but with just as much inner resolve she began what for her was the arduous and disruptive task of having a child. It took years to accomplish and cost her the pain and exhaustion of several miscarriages, yet she was determined to make this personal act as a defiance, however irrational, in the face of those infant murders and distortions she could do nothing about.

Consider the strange family history of the Tolstoys. Here is a case of the failure of that catalytic action children often provide for their parents. The whole process of parenthood was rejected and despised as a constant reminder of weakness and failed ideals.

Leo Tolstoy married late, after having lived the life of an aristocratic Russian rake. He was thirty-four, almost twice the age of Sonya, his eighteen-year-old bride. Approaching mid-life, he had been seized by a desire to re-create his own happy childhood memories at his large country estate, Yasnaya Polanya. "The whole house will be run along the same lines as in my father's day; we'll begin the same life all over again, but with a change of roles," he wrote. "I'll take my father's place.... My wife will take my mother's place, and the children will take ours."

After his marriage, however, his mercurial nature failed to take on the stolidity of his father's. Here was a man who had everything the nineteenth century had to offer: wealth, power, land, intellect, moral sensitivity. Yet he appeared unable to settle down and put these gifts to good use. He cast about with a whole list of projects he wanted to accomplish, from educating the peasants who farmed his land to writing avant-garde plays for the Moscow Little Theatre. He and his young wife even took up the questionable habit of each keeping diaries which the other could read any time, hoping to achieve the ideal of complete honesty with another human soul. The diaries, however, only became weapons to use against one another, and their result was more often hysteria than honesty.

The second year brought the birth of their first son. But Tolstoy found that the birth brought him neither joy nor pride, only a vague sense of unease, as though there would now be "another area of vulnerability" in his life. Indeed, only a few days before his son was born, Tolstoy revealed his dread of this new incursion into his autonomy, writing in his dairy, "Where is it—my old self, the self I loved and knew, who still springs to the surface sometimes and pleases and frightens me? I have become petty and insignificant."

Nevertheless, within a few months he had finally begun work on what was to be an undertaking of tremendous proportions, the novel *War and Peace*. Would his "old self" have been able to concentrate sufficiently to carry through with this monumental project? Did this little nucleus, this little crystal of a family, cause the accretion of his powers around a controlling center? At any rate, he became so absorbed in this work that his scattered energies unified themselves and his emotions achieved a balance they never had at any other point in his life. The entries in his diary dwindled away until he finally closed it, not opening it again for thirteen years, during which period he completed both *War and Peace* and *Anna Karenina*.

Do we attribute this sudden surge in organized creativity,

this amazing new stability, to Tolstoy's becoming a family man? The answer is ambiguous.

For one thing, Tolstoy, although he fathered thirteen children in marriage, was never really a family man. Only ten days before the birth of his seventh son, he approached his bishop about the possibility of becoming a monk. He could never get over the feeling that his purity was somehow sullied by marriage and children. He refused to be drawn into the mundane concerns of managing his large household, making provision for his children, and overseeing their education, although he found time to absorb himself in the lives of the peasants and to learn the craft of cobbling shoes, a task he took to be properly humble and uncompromising to his ethics. All business and family matters devolved upon his wife whom he then repeatedly rebuked for her impious materialism and for taking too much thought for the things of this world. Yet he himself, while dressing up and playacting the peasant and switching from one spiritual diet to another, continued to live off the proceeds of Sonya's business acumen.

Disappointed in his sons because they showed no ambition to carry on his work of reforming the conscience of the nation, Tolstoy wrote, "It would have been better for me to have no children at all." He despised his daughters' desires to marry and wrote to the first one who did the following fatherly advice: "You must have guessed that your decision means failure to me; you know it full well, but on the other hand I am glad to think that it will be easier for you to live after abandoning your ideal, or rather after mingling your ideal with baser aspirations, by which I mean having children."

It was not unusual for parents to lose several children in death during the nineteenth century. What was unusual was the manner in which Tolstoy accepted these losses. Upon the death of a young son he wrote, "There is some consolation in the fact that of the eight of us, his death was certainly the easiest for us all to bear. . . ." And even his daughter Masha, who gratified him in his later years by taking up his philosophical principles and whom he called "the one I love best of all those around me," evoked this notice in his diary when she died at thirty-five: "November 29, 1906. They have just taken her away, carried her off to be buried.

Thank God, I am not depressed." And when another son died, a boy of four, he was able to write in a supercilious tone, "My wife has been much afflicted by this death and I, too, am sorry that the little boy I loved is no longer here, but despair is only for those who shut their eyes to the commandments by which we are ruled."

Nonetheless, in a sense, Tolstoy's children did indeed act as a catalyst that forced a serious reconsideration of his spiritual enterprise. They were, for one thing, living remonstrances against his uncontrollable sensuality, his divided nature. Whereas Augustine had put off his own conversion because of his similar fears that he could not maintain his chastity, he had finally accepted that Christ would have to fight the battle for him. Tolstoy, on the other hand, continued in his divided state until his death, year after year piling up a brood that was only a reproach and burden to him and that he could never fully love.

It was only after his two great novels were finished and when his oldest children were nearly grown that Tolstoy had his spiritual awakening. He who had spent a good part of his life rejecting the orthodox faith of his fathers now threw himself into exercises of piety in order to "be united with my ancestors and fellow men and continue my search for the meaning of life." But the reconciliation of this middle-aged prodigal with the faith of his family did not last. He could not, it seems, be united with his ancestors without also accepting his own fatherhood. In less than two years he had once again begun his attack on the church, not this time from the point of view of a worldly agnostic, but by establishing his own version of Christianity.

There was nothing particularly new about his version, although it turned out to have a wide appeal to other guilt-ridden liberal intellectuals of his day. It was founded on a return to the simple life and the Sermon on the Mount, while abjuring all ecclesiastical doctrine and dogma. "What Tolstoy really wanted," says his biographer Henri Troyat, "was to believe in God and to live according to Christian morality, while denying the divinity of Christ." And, revealingly, the doctrines that most stuck in the Tolstoyan craw were first, that of the Trinity, involving the eternal relationship between the Father, the Son, and the Spirit, and second, that of the Incarnation through the fleshly birth.

His new-found belief, however, brought him no relief from his divided nature. All over Russia young students and intellectuals were founding "Tolstoy communities." He was regarded a veritable prophet, honored even in his own country, yet he himself could not find the wherewithal to live by his own ideals. He lived, therefore, an exile among his own family, constantly threatening to run away from home to live the pure life of the peasantry, but never able to bring himself to that point. All he could do was to wear a muzhik's blouse and adopt a vegetarian diet.

His family was bewildered by his new course. His wife, for whom the Orthodox Church provided religion sufficient to her needs, told him, "You used to be worried because you had no faith; why aren't you happy now that you have it?" And his second son, Ilya, wrote:

> From the fun-loving, lively head of our family he was trans-
> formed before our eyes into a stern accusatory prophet. . . .
> We would be planning an amateur play, everybody was
> animated, chatting away, playing croquet, talking of love,
> etc. Papa appeared and with one word, or worse, one look,
> everything was spoiled: the gaiety was gone; we felt
> ashamed, somehow. It would have been better for him to
> stay away.

This terrible conflict with his family went on for the rest of Tolstoy's long life. It was only at the age of eighty-two, a few days before his death, that he finally plucked up the courage to run away from home. Having by then converted only one member of his family, his daughter Sasha, to Tolstoyism, he relied on her to help spirit him from the house one winter dawn. Thus the old man, sick and sometimes wandering in his mind, made his final flight from his family.

It was a journey that became an allegory of his whole life. First he fled to a monastery, of all places, close by the convent where his aged sister was a nun. He spent a day and a night there in great peace, even making plans to settle in a peasant's hut nearby. But the past could not be buried quite so simply, nor the unreconciled conflicts that had torn his life be so easily forgotten. His daughter appeared suddenly at the convent, and, startled from his cover, his decision veered again. Fearing that the rest of his family might find him there, too, he set off once more aboard a train. He rapidly became too sick to travel further and had to be put to bed in a railway station. There he died, in the extravagant circumstances only a Russian could devise, surrounded by the international press and film crews, yet cut off from all his family except the one daughter, who refused to let even her mother in to see him.

What is to be made of this man at once so powerful and so weak, so torn between his self-constructed ideals and the reality of family life that bore in upon him and became more repugnant every day? He could not have been entirely lacking in what we call natural affections. His children's sustained fondness for him, even in the face of conflict, attests to that. The letter he wrote to his son Ilya before his marriage is full of tenderness, truth, and good sense. And though he greatly resented the intrusion of other personalities into his realm of autonomy, he was equally delicate about intruding into his children's lives.

His children were indeed a spiritual catalyst for him. One way and another they never ceased to worry him, like an aching tooth or a strange code that he couldn't quite decipher. First, they refused to realize his early hopes of replicating his own happy childhood. Later they balked at following him through his spiritual conversion.

But Tolstoy was never glad for the transformation his offspring produced in him. He would have much preferred to keep himself inviolate. He had no desire to be a mere link in a chain, a connection between the past and the future. He wanted to be the whole show, entire of himself. If he had not the option of remaining physically virginal, he at any rate hoped to maintain his spiritual virginity by not allowing any outside element to invade his autonomy, by resisting any change outside his control. With thirteen children and a strong-willed wife, small wonder the man was in continual conflict.

It is easy enough to sympathize with Tolstoy's divided nature, foreshadowing as it does the current expectations of modern family life. The initial easy nostalgia for the past. The age-old desire to make one's children replicas of oneself, coupled with the contradictory desire to remain inviolate, to draw an "area of unvulnerability" around oneself where one can act with impunity without fear of the long, hidden consequences of one's life upon another's or theirs upon yours. And finally the quite understandable and natural desire to throw off the shackles of parenthood.

The conflict we see in Tolstoy is precisely the conflict we see in ourselves, the struggle between autonomous selfhood and the subjugation of will that family inevitably means. This is not new, however, this chafing at the communal bit. The twentieth century did not invent it, although we are intent on inventing as much justifying jargon for it as possible. Whereas Tolstoy was straightforward and precise in describing his divided nature— even, as someone has said, daring to take notes under the very nose of God—our own descriptions are vague and sentimental as rationalizations tend to be. We talk of giving our children only quality time so as to devote more energy to developing our own potential, as though human life could be dehydrated and concentrated in order to avoid the dull spots.

One has only to look at the covert evidence contained in our literature to see that as a nation we have never much valued family life as fulfillment. Whereas England has its great chroniclers of domesticity—Jane Austen, Charles Dickens, Thackeray, Galsworthy—we have never had a major writer to tell us, as Samuel Johnson put it, "To be happy at home is the end of all human endeavor." On the contrary, American writers have been much more in agreement with Tolstoy who began *Anna Karenina* with the inaccurate and cynical statement, "Happy families are all alike; every unhappy family is unhappy in its own way."

From James Fenimore Cooper and his solitary hero, Natty Bumppo, through Hawthorne's ill-starred Hester Prynne and Melville's resolutely isolated Captain Ahab, to Twain's fugitives from society and Hemingway who found it necessary to kill off both the children and wives of his adventurers, there has never been a complete, intact, happy family in American literature. It has not even been a mythical ideal, except for the Bobbsey twins. Even Nancy Drew was a motherless child. For Homer and Dickens happiness might have been the reunion of the family after many tribulations, but in America our heroes, starting with Daniel Boone, have always been in search of "elbow room."

The family has simply failed to capture our imaginations. The exceptions to this, of course, are those for whom the maintaining of the family has been a constant striving, an almost unattainable ideal offering as much challenge to their ingenuity as the pursuit of a white whale or a raft trip down the Mississippi. *Roots,* for example, did indeed capture our imaginations because of the enormity of the effort required to defend the family from threat.

We may have national conferences about the problems of families. Sunday supplements may be full of features about what is happening to the American family. Sociologists may ponder statistics trying to track the mutations in this phenomenon. But as long as that human undertaking we call the family fails to capture the imagination of our culture, as long as the solitary explorer, the single shopper for lifestyles, the misunderstood mercenary or artist remain the only kind of heroes we acknowledge, there's not really much chance for a change in our perspective. We will all be like Tolstoy, impatient of constraints on our autonomy, using our very idealism to excuse us from the irritations of domesticity.

In the end it comes down to a choice between accepting a certain porousness and insisting upon a definite impermeability. Between becoming a piece of limestone, through which life flows and filters, genes sluicing from the unalterable past into the uncontrollable millrace of the future, and becoming impenetrable chalcedony refusing imprint. A choice between the interstices of one's being clogged with the contingencies and consequences of other lives and a polished, impervious self-containment.

Given a choice, God knows I too would have chosen the still, cold center of myself, safe from the flaws that the carelessness of others could inflict upon my surface. Aesthetically it certainly has more appeal. If one sets out to create one's life, one surely wants a goodly amount of artistic control over the results. Admitting other people into the process invariably means messiness. A collapse of intention here, a flood of exuberance there that recedes to leave behind the wreck and residues of failure.

Taking up a family, on the other hand, is a good deal like consenting to become a fossil, itself a peculiar kind of earthen vessel. Fossils are made by the slow replacement of organic material with minerals. The hard structures of a living thing dissolve and are simultaneously replaced by other substances, pyrite or hematite silica. The original organism has no control over the results. But the process does leave behind evidence of life forms for our contemplation.

Fortunately I wasn't given the chance to choose. Married at the last moment in history before women were widely supplied with that chemical barricade in the bloodstream, that contraceptive seine that strains out imprudent reproductive possibilities, I found myself at twenty-two with two strange interlopers in my life. The dissolution of my hard structures began, and the space they left was infiltrated by these new, unaccountable substances. As bewildered as Tolstoy, I had become the unwitting agency of life.

CHAPTER NINE

The Mirror of Nature

I watched a television program last night about birth. It began with incredible shots of an ovary exploding like a detonated minefield at the release of a single egg cell. Twenty-two years ago I should have felt just such an internal explosion going off inside my own body at the approach of what was to prove not just a catalytic but a cataclysmic event in my life. Biology, Freud said, is destiny. And in my case he was right, although not perhaps in the sense he intended. For by two such unmarked internal eruptions, miniscule quakes unregistered and unnoticed for weeks, was my destiny determined. They altered my life forever.

I never wanted to have children. I had an exciting career already fantasized for myself right out of American literature—full of metaphoric trips down the Mississippi and voyages in search of mythic beasts. Domesticity all but disgusted me. Motherhood was a trap into which only the unwary fell. I had acquired a husband, but we were both agreed on the value of a life unencumbered by reproduction. Hardly more than children ourselves, we had not yet waked from the wide-eyed dreaming of adolescence.

Margaret Mead records that she had always had an innate affection for children. As a girl she loved taking care of smaller children and wanted to have six of her own when she grew up. I had absolutely no such natural maternal instincts to go on. I had always been bored with babies, beginning with my own little brother. At the discovery of my first pregnancy, I was frightened and infuriated. I came home from the doctor's office and cried. I called my parents and cried. I spent the next several months literally sodden with self-pity. There was nothing natural about me.

But what is natural in such cases? When we look at the evidence from that world we call nature, we find such a varied display of behavior that hardly any parental activity seems unnatural. Most animals never even acknowledge their own offspring. From single-celled paramecium to insects and up to the reptile families, children are nothing more to their parents than an increase in the competition for food. Sometimes they even become part of the food supply.

The care-taking function of parents begins to appear among animals somewhere around the level of spiders. Few fish or reptiles, either male or female, go to any trouble over their offspring. Most of the species in these groups lay large numbers of eggs and then leave them to fend for themselves. However, as organisms become more complex, their offspring seem to be more dependent at birth and to need their parents' care for a longer period of time. Just how this care is provided, though, varies greatly within classes of animals.

All birds and mammals provide some care for their offspring. There are, of course, some birds who turn their children over to others to care for, the most notorious of these being the cuckoo.

What makes this sort of foster-parenting possible is a phenomenon known as "imprinting." This is a little understood process by which adult and child are seemingly bonded together almost irrevocably by early, initial exposure to one another. Whomever the baby first opens its eyes on, no matter how improbable the impostor, becomes the parent. For some ducklings and goslings, any large, moving object will do, including a human being.

It seems impossible for any adult bird, once it is fatally imprinted, to resist its nestlings' charming gestures of dependency. The parent's response to the gawky movements and insistent cries of whatever progeny fills the nest is immediate and tender. Herring gull chicks even seem to catch on to their parents' weakness and, as they near the age when they will be ejected from the nest, actually try to chirp baby-gull talk and hunker down in the nest, pulling in their necks to look smaller.

As we trace the increasing complexity of organisms up the ladder of living things, we find that nature becomes less profligate in the production of sexual cells that have the capacity to become extensions of the species. Insects and fish lay huge numbers of eggs and leave them to survive as best they can. Birds lay only a few eggs and provide more care for those few. Within the mammal group, litters become smaller as the organism becomes more complex, until with the primates there is usually only one offspring produced per mating.

The survival of this single offspring demands more extended and deliberate care. A single-celled infant *Ciliata* has exactly as much equipment and competence for dealing with its environment and surviving as its parent cell. But a newborn kitten must be cleaned up, fed, kept warm, and shielded from the light by its mother for a good many weeks. A young lion must be trained by its kin how to hunt, dismember, and defend its food. A rhesus monkey must learn its proper place in the stratification of privilege and responsibility that make up its social structure.

A lion pride is perhaps the most child-centered family to be found in that world we call nature. Taking care of the young engages not just the mother but the entire social group. When there are no babies among them, the older animals in the pride

grow intolerant of one another. Fights continually break out between males trying to establish dominance. Adolescents are robbed
of their food. All is snarling and bickering. Many pregnant females
wisely go off by themselves to whelp into dense underbrush away
from this inhospitable environment. After about ten weeks, however, the mothers lead their large-eyed cubs out of the thickets and
introduce them to the group of adults. Immediately all fighting
and tensions end. Tenderness descends on every lion heart. Even
the aging animals with aching bones are gentle in their rebuffs of
the rowdy youngsters. The mother lions happily baby-sit with each
other's offspring. The pride becomes one great playschool where
the adults patiently teach physical dexterity and hunting skills to
the young.

Of course adolescence eventually catches up with the cubs.
By the time they are eighteen months old their charm is wearing a
little thin for the grownups. Their mothers are once again expecting and no longer help them hunt or save tidbits for them. For the
one almost universal rule among animal families is that childhood
ends. Creatures may vary, by nature, as to their reproductive rituals and the care, if any, that they give their young; but the one
ironclad rule for all is the rejection, at some point, of the offspring.
They are turned out of the nest, driven off, sometimes even eaten.
When the door shuts between childhood and adulthood in the
animal kingdom, it locks forever. Mother Nature and Father Time
form an uncompromising alliance. In nature, no father ever waits
for the return of the prodigal.

Biological clocks govern all these various kinds of reproductive and parental behavior. Fertility periods, gestation lengths,
imprinting perimeters are all limited. Only during certain critical
periods can the basic social behavior characteristic of its species be
established in a young animal. A lamb or a kid has only four hours
to get itself accepted by its mother. After that period, her rejection
is final and absolute. And these early behavior patterns, usually
involving the necessary intimacy between mother and child, are
later limited by another biological alarm which signals childhood's
end.

When human parents begin their long and arduous pil-
grimage with their children, they often have a hard time seeing

that this state will not last forever. In fact, the number of nights spent caring for a sick child or the seemingly endless procession of school programs, soccer games, and music lessons is actually finite. In a sense they will be parents to the end of their days, but at some point that parenthood will diminish and become almost vestigial. In about twenty years, less than one-third of a life span, most mothers and fathers are done with the job. The clock runs down. There is a point where even the possibility of having more children disappears.

No species, of course, has the capacity for making reproduction and child-rearing so unnatural as humans. We can chemically disrupt the body's natural rhythm of fertility until it suits our purposes to do otherwise. We can physically obstruct the frantic assault of spermatazoa upon the ovum. We can either avert or allow the implantation of a fertilized ovum in the uterus. We can choose to abort an already implanted fetus. We are not driven to do any of these things by animal instincts. We intentionally choose them. Intention is in fact what makes us unnatural, what separates us from the rest of creation.

Not that barriers to reproduction do not occur in the animal kingdom. Some unions are naturally barren. Spontaneous abortions can afflict whole herds of cattle. Rabbit mothers can reabsorb their would-be bunnies back into their own systems if their diet is sparse or if they are sufficiently frightened. Certain birds in North America have tottered on the verge of extinction because pesticides they have unwittingly eaten have made the shells of their eggs too thin and fragile to hold developing chicks. Even infanticide is not unnatural. One only has to watch guppies gobble up their progeny or tomcats stalk their own young to see "natural" population control in action.

I had been reading books on animal families, intrigued by the bizarre behavior found among them, when it suddenly struck me one evening that all these myriad manners among animals, foreign as they may sometimes seem, reflect the varieties of behavior in the human species. The parental behavior of most warm-blooded animals may strike us as more "natural" than the indifference of cold-blooded creatures to their children. But to our everlasting shame, we are not always such dependable parents as the lions or even the herring gulls. If we find the cuckoo's abandonment of their children odious, it is only because we have seen it among our own kind. No behavior found in beasts is actually alien to us; we, the apex of animals, embrace them all.

We also go beyond them. We have something we call free will. True, we still have internal biological clocks, just like the rest of the beasts. But we also have means of resetting them, of turning them off altogether, or of simply ignoring their insistent ringing. Puberty, for example, with its biological clamoring, happens to just about everybody. But in industrialized society we have determined to put a damper on that roaring furnace demanding reproduction of the organism. We stretch adolescence to the breaking point with the contradictory demands of the economy, education, and national defense because we are unwilling to subject these specifically human activities to the tyranny of biology.

I have said I was not a "natural" mother. But perhaps I was a type of the most natural of mothers. The unchoosing. The unprepared. The unplanned parent.

I was as surprised at the advent of our offspring as our adolescent cat was at her first litter. She wandered about the house, dropping kittens in the most inappropriate places and mewling in pained bewilderment. But maternity took hold of both of us in due course. She had to be forced to wean her second batch of kittens, and I was so deeply imprinted with my daughters that I could detect a change in their breathing through two walls in the middle of the night fast asleep. I did not choose to become a mother, but once I was, the imprint was indelible. Even today, with both my children gone, it only takes a twitch on the telephone line to undo me and all my plans.

These girls come home from college and sprawl across my bed where I'm trying to read at night. They even bring their roommates and friends. There they like to narrate their lives to me, especially the parts that are confusing to them. They still giggle, although their laughter, on the far side of adolescence now, often has that adult, ironic edge to it. They ask me if I think they're gaining weight, if they should cut their hair, why good men are so hard to find, if they should change their major, why philosophy is so impractical, what the meaning of 1 Thessalonians 4:13 is. My responses are usually more or less inarticulate mother-sounds—groans, sighs, snorts, interjections of amazement or skepticism.

I feel swamped with all this youthful flesh surrounding me, awash in a sea of long, lithely muscled legs, unwrinkled kneecaps, improbable eyelashes, French braids, frizzed permanents, innocent elbows.

Propped on my pillow on the edge of the bed nearest the reading lamp, I grip my book like an anchor. All unaware, they are calling up the imprint; like invisible but indelible ink it emerges. I cannot even resist the roommates. They are like the herring gull chicks, pulling in their necks, widening their eyes, making baby cries, in order to be let back into the nest. Giggling and bouncing and snuggling, they want, for a little longer, reassurance, refuge, unction.

And I, in my divided nature, hold my book in one hand and a daughter's shoulder in the other as she nestles her head into my lap. I could say this represents the struggle between the me and the not-me, between the needs of the autonomous individual and the demands of the offspring. But that would not be quite accurate. Because I have a need for them as much as they for me.

This tangle of arms and legs and these offhand questions about eternal verities, this Sargasso Sea of clinging child-weeds, is a rich feeding ground for me too. For despite the fact that half of all the genetic material in every chromosome in every cell in their bodies has been bequeathed to them by me, an instruction manual they must follow whether they will or not, they are as rare and curious to me as if they had come from the ends of the earth. I feel like Marco Polo discovering marvels and prodigies. They have always been thus to me, conundrums that have dropped undeciphered from the sky. I have no need of UFOs or interplanetary travelers to mystify me. I have these daughters. (They will find this confession "passing strange" since I tell them frequently and with equal sincerity that I know them better than they know themselves.)

I have always needed them, and not just as grist for some private intellectual mill. There have been times in my life when their imprint was the only code I had to cling to. My being was branded, scored, seared with maternal obligation, and that alone provided me with a certainty stable enough to keep me from capsizing altogether. However the world may have muddled me, whatever else I may not have known, I did know this much: that I was responsible for the care of two small human beings. If I had not been cut adrift from their helplessness, I would have sunk sooner than they.

My own motherhood may be nothing more than my in-stinctual response to the imprinting that occurred when my daughter and I first looked at one another like the sole survivors of a shipwreck. If the truth be known, I may not have actually chosen to procreate or to caretake any more than a goose or a gibbon. And I can hardly claim credit for any particular virtue associated with maternity. My own righteousness does not reside in what I cannot in any case help.

But if our taking care of one another, young and old, is to go beyond those examples we find among the animals, then we need a pattern that nature alone cannot complete. As imitators of a heavenly Father who never abandons his children, more is asked of us than a few years of nursery-tending. Still, the pattern begins in nature. There we see its first faint outlines. And while we are striving toward the completion of that pattern, let us not forget our lowly nature nor despise our kinship with the beasts. We are still a part of creation. Let us learn to give thanks for that. When Jesus went through the wilderness, both the angels and the wild beasts were with him. It is the Father for whom all families on earth are named who made us all.

CHAPTER TEN

The Leaky Ark

Nature serves us as a many-faceted mirror. We see reflected there our own forms of family life. Not only the protecting father and the nurturing mother, but, alas, the absconding parent, the murderous mate.

But this mirror has its limitations. Not quite all possible family forms are exhibited by lower species. We can see a progression in both complexity and quality of behavior from, say, an oyster bed to a rhesus monkey tribe. Therefore we should expect to find a corresponding increase of social involvement in ourselves. There is a point at which we transcend the higher primates, just as a giraffe transcends a jellyfish.

For one thing, the length of our caretaking is greatly extended past the average upper mammalian limits of two years. By two a human child is still nowhere near being able to find food for itself, nor to care with any competency for its other needs. Puberty does not descend on human children for a dozen or more years, and even then full physical development is not complete for a good many more. In other words, family life, based on no more than physical dependency, is greatly drawn out among human beings. Nowhere in nature can we find a parallel for this lengthy relationship necessary for human families, nor for the quality of conscious participation in shaping behavior.

It is necessary, then, to go beyond nature to grasp the scope of human families. Where shall we go?

We may compare one human family to another. We can look at Margaret Mead's Mundugumors alongside Charles Dickens's Micawbers, turn over the Tolstoys or the Kierkegaards for clues as to our capacities. But how do we know which family is headed toward its proper destiny? Unless we have some totally other source, some code from outside our own frame of reference, we seem likely to go on spinning on the axis of our own chromosomes' double helices.

So let us move now from nature to revelation, or at least to revelation's residue, scorched and scored into what we call Scripture. What do we discover about the human family here? As a history of generations shaping and sustaining one another, what does the Bible have to offer us?

The original article, for one thing. Adam and Eve. Not a very promising beginning. A couple like Bonnie and Clyde, partners first in crime and later in pain and toil. Cain and Abel. The fruit of that first travail a murderer of his own brother and consequently a fugitive. Then finally the child of consolation, Seth, to take the place of the murdered Abel.

But Seth was a long time coming. Probably over a hundred years. No doubt he prefigures not only the long wait of Sarah and Abraham for the promised Isaac, but also the deferred hopes of many other human parents.

Cain was a bitter disappointment to those first parents. But ironically he also became the archetype of the son who makes good.

He had, of course, to give up the agricultural interests that had caused him so much grief to begin with; he had to pull up roots, so to speak, and set out toward the land of Nod, a marked man. There his fortunes took a turn for the better. He went into real-estate development, and by the time his first son, Enoch, was born, he was able to name a city after him. There must have been a good many more talents buried in those genes, too, because it was Cain's descendants who were credited with inventing musical instruments and composition, metal work and animal husbandry. All the fruits of civilization come down to us from a fratricide.

Seth stayed at home and was apparently not so ambitious as his older brother. But he did have children—none of them very remarkable until we get to Noah. By that time the population was exploding and with it the crime statistics. Only Noah seemed to be worth saving from the watery grave God had planned as a means of washing the world clean again. But saving Noah alone, making him into a biblical Robinson Crusoe, was obviously not sufficient. So Noah's wife, his three sons and their wives had to be included in the compact. Salvaging a solitary individual with no prospects for spinning out that twisted thread of complex protein molecules we call life would have made little sense.

We have largely lost the sense of immortality achieved through reproduction that the ancients relied upon. But Israel did not assimilate a notion of spiritualized immortality until rather late in their history. Before that, one's future life was primarily a projection of one's genetic material forward into future time. Nor was this belief ever totally abandoned. The Sadducees in Jesus' time still insisted upon this sort of immortality as the only valid one.

At the outset of each of the Bible's main narrative sections following the Flood—the patriarchal history, the formation of the nation, and the account of the monarchy—there is a story about either a miraculous birth or the rescue of a child from threatening danger. In the patriarchal history there is a child of promise, Isaac, whose own parents had trouble at times believing in his arrival. Abraham, in fact, despairing of descendants, had already provided himself with an adopted legal heir, Eliezer of Damascus. And Sarah, shamed by her barrenness, cooked up the disastrous plot to provide her maid Hagar as a surrogate mother for the promised heir. Isaac's very name was inspired by disbelieving laughter. And later, after the promise had been delivered, there was the terrible moment when the One who had given the miraculous child—this only hope of immortality, this purposed ancestor of star-numbered offspring—seemed about to snatch him away again.

When it was time for Abraham's descendants to be forged into a nation, Moses, the intended agency for this task, was threatened with early extinction at the hands of Pharaoh's soldiers. Only his concealment and safeguarding by his mother and sister, and later by Pharaoh's own daughter, made the establishment of the nation of Israel possible.

And the child Samuel, again the gift granted to a childless woman, became the tool used to ordain (however unwillingly) the monarchy. He was the one on whom the Lord's Spirit rested, the one who searched out and anointed the chosen kings of Israel.

These tales of menaced childhoods, of babies that barely got born, show us just how precarious a thing destiny is. These stories underscore the danger that destiny is constantly subjected to, and in that danger we can taste a little of the flavor families had for the Hebrews. We can see why barrenness was such a reproach to the women, why heirs were so important, why Sarah was willing to substitute Hagar for herself to provide a son. Only children could insure one's continued participation in the destiny of eternal purpose. Only through propagation could one achieve any form of immortality.

"One generation shall praise thy works to another." Each generation was a conscious strand of DNA, informing the next with the knowledge recorded in its memory. Just as a greater portion of caretaking becomes conscious with human parents, so the replication of information from one generation to the next becomes a conscious, rather than a merely chemical, act.

Of course, it didn't always work out that way, even for the Israelites. The transmission didn't always take place. Parents may indeed have praised the Lord's works to their children, but that didn't insure that the children paid much attention. Adam and Eve at least taught their two boys to acknowledge their Maker. But somewhere along the line Cain must have missed a vital connection. If Abel got the message straight, why didn't Cain? That remains the mystery at the core of parenthood. The story of Cain and Abel must be right there at the beginning of that long, sad tale of humanity so that parents don't get their hopes up. Or rather so that their hopes are not misplaced. The world's first threatened child was not rescued. The best odds we can count on for our own children listening to our instruction is one in two. The only hope in that story is in the mercy shown to the murderer.

By the time of Noah the odds had gotten even worse. Of all the earth's population, apparently Noah was the only one who still carried the correct conscious code for communing with the Creator. Current genetics textbooks tell us that the random sorting of chromosomes is a matter of chance. Be that as it may, and given the fact that all three of Noah's sons were with him in the ark and experienced the same deliverance as he did, the world picture did not improve markedly after the Flood. However the chromosomes and the consciousness got sorted out among those three sons, it doesn't seem to have upgraded the behavior of the general populace. This first experiment in eugenics seems to have been a failure.

Scholars call the first eleven chapters of Genesis the primeval history. It is supposed to give us an idea of the sorry shape the human race has been in from the beginning. The rest of Genesis is devoted to what is called the patriarchal history. As the name implies, this is where the Author of the saga really got serious about using the family as a means of transmitting knowledge of himself. From Abraham on, producing offspring became the consuming passion of these particular people. Children were the very content of God's promise to this wandering Aramean— divinely planned parenthood on a cosmic scale.

There was no misapprehending the Lord's intentions this time. It was specifically through Abraham and his descendants that the knowledge of God would be spread to all the earth's inhabitants. The family was to be the primary means of transmitting that information. Instead of entering the ark this time, the family would itself *be* the ark, the carrier of the code that explains life itself.

Did it work? Again the answer is ambiguous. That family, begun so inauspiciously, is still going strong today, thousands of years later. But its performance, taken at any isolated moment in history, could often be judged a failure. Certainly while Abraham's descendants languished as the ignorant slaves of a much more sophisticated and stable civilization, no one would have believed them the ones entrusted with the secret code. Nor later while they straggled across the desert, against their will, complaining every step of the way to the Promised Land.

The family proved a leaky vessel at best in which to store such a valuable cargo. Abraham himself seems to have been a weak-kneed sort, bartering his bride to the local bully every time he trespassed on someone else's territory. It's fortunate that Abraham's faith was counted to him as righteousness. He certainly hadn't much inherent virtue to go on. And his faith was sporadic enough at best. It gave him the initial bravado to set out from Haran, but it couldn't withstand the famine in Canaan. Nor the temptation of using the slave woman Hagar as a surrogate source of an heir.

Still, despite Abraham's wavering, God is faithful to his promise. The child was delivered. The stage seemed set for a happy ending. Then, into this story of the primal patriarch came that most terrible doom, the offstage voice demanding the life of the child as forfeit. Could the leaks in the vessel only be caulked with the blood of his own son? Child sacrifice was not unknown in the land where he lived. Other gods demanded it. Why not this one? Surely the higher the price one pays, the stronger the god one buys. But to Abraham, the sacrifice of his son would have meant not only the end of himself but the end of any conscious connection between the story and its Author, the end of any partnership between the Creator and his characters.

But Isaac was spared. And the story moved on, down the line of his descendants, to Esau and Jacob, brothers at war even in the womb. Here is our first example of family intrigue. It was instigated by a doting mother whose favorite is the younger child. There is enough deception, chicanery, and plain greed in this part of the story to satisfy the demands of any modern soap opera. In family relationships, Jacob is not a morally edifying hero. Neither as a brother or a son, nor even later as a father, is he a great success. He takes advantage of Esau's slower wits, lies to his father, and creates dissension among his own sons by making Joseph his minion. Small wonder Joseph's older brothers were willing to sell him into slavery, this spoiled sibling who flaunted his favored position in the family.

It is true that, at the end of the patriarchal history, we are given an almost Dickensian dénouement. There is the family, all wrongs righted, all grievances forgiven, reunited in Egypt. Joseph smiles benignly on all his brothers, having finally become the fairytale prince he had always dreamed himself to be. The picture is complete. The ark is safe and staunch. The descendants are becoming so numerous by now that even the random sorting of chromosomes seems no longer a problem. The genetic pool has grown so wide and deep that there will always be a statistical certainty, a saving remnant if you will, to carry the code.

But as it turns out, this is only a momentary interlude in the story; it serves to mortise the tale of a family to that of a nation. It takes only the space of a breath to turn the page from the final deathbed scene in Genesis to the next episode of the Exodus. But it took the Israelites four hundred long years to live it. During those centuries the descendants of Jacob did nothing remarkable except proliferate. They filled the land. (The Egyptians were understandably nervous.)

Here the story itself takes another tack; it begins to use other devices than the tracing of the family tree. Following the genealogical thread of the story had worked well when each patriarch had only managed to produce one primary heir, with the secondary sons like Ishmael and Esau thrown in as foils to their brothers. But after Jacob fathered twelve sons it became impossible to shape that many multiple lines into a manageable study. Thus the main action shifts to Moses. A comparatively insignificant member of Levi's branch of the family.

Once again, with the beginning of a new episode, the child destined to be the deliverer of his people is threatened with early extinction. And despite the disappearance of the patriarchs from the scene, the family still provides the ark, quite literally this time, for salvaging the nascent carrier of the God-code, the one who will one day face the Lord for the whole nation.

It was Moses' mother who got the papyrus basket and

caulked it with tar and pitch and set him among the reeds in the river. It was his sister Miriam who stood watch over him and beguiled the Egyptian princess first to adopt him and then to use his own mother for a wet-nurse. It was that surrogate Egyptian mother who protected him until adulthood. And when Moses returned from his desert exile, it was his brother Aaron whom he sought out to speak for him. Thus the family, dispossessed, despoiled, beggared as it was of its rightful strength and structures, still provided shelter and succor for Israel's savior.

However, it was that same brother Aaron and sister Miriam, the ones who led the celebration after the defeat of the Egyptians, who also rebelled against their brother Moses in the wilderness and set the people against him. Such are the unavoidable ambiguities of families. The final twist in the ironies of this particular family is that when the Lord resolved to punish these unruly siblings, Moses took their part against God himself.

Sibling rivalry, starting with the first pair of brothers, appears as a constant theme throughout all these stories: Cain and Abel; Esau and Jacob; Joseph and his brothers; Aaron, Miriam, and Moses; the young David and his brothers; David's own warring sons.

It is almost as frequent a theme as the rebellion of child against parent. Among these examples, one would again have to count Cain, the original prodigal; Noah's son Ham who ridiculed his father's weakness; Jacob who took advantage of his father's failing senses to steal his brother's rightful blessing; the eleven sons of Jacob who convinced their father that his favorite son was dead; the sons of the prophet-priests, Eli and Samuel, who brought disgrace upon their office. And worst of all, the sons of David: Amnon who raped his sister and was murdered by his brother, and Absalom who would have deposed and murdered his father the king.

Indeed, it becomes very hard to find a happy family in these stories. One searches for other happy endings, even a happy moment, a fleeting tableau where the family members are united and at peace with one another. Abraham's descendants, the gene pool through which all people on earth were to be blessed by the knowledge of God they carried, had become a veritable ocean by now. But the knowledge was also greatly diluted and adulterated. It still broke out here and there in odd places—in a stutterer like Moses, a dull-witted athlete like Samson, or a fig-pruner like Amos—but its movement, its manifestation, seemed as unpredictable as the appearance of recessive genetic traits.

If we look to these stories for illustrations of happy families, we are going to be greatly disappointed. What few we find are no more than fragments. Recall the infrequent instances, if you will, of family felicity. There were Noah's other two sons, Shem and Japheth, so careful of their father's dignity, despite his disreputable drunken behavior, that they covered him up while deferentially averting their eyes. Or Uncle Abraham allowing his nephew Lot to choose the best grazing lands and then later rescuing the ingrate from the bad company that went along with the good life in Sodom. And we have already mentioned the craft by which Moses' mother and sister insured his survival.

Then there was Hannah, humiliated when her fervent prayer for a child was mistaken by Eli as drunkenness, but nonetheless persevering until she was promised a pregnancy. Even so, she only had a couple of years to keep the child. Like the fairy-tale queen who had promised her baby to the dwarf Rumpelstiltskin, Hannah treasured the infant Samuel all the more for his having been so hard to come by. But the Bible is no fairy tale. The queen outwitted the malevolent dwarf, but Hannah had to fulfill her bargain and hand her son over to the priest.

Another tableau of family affection is made up of Naomi and Ruth, leaning on one another as they make their way back from Moab to Bethlehem. It is a favorite subject among Sunday school illustrators. The bitter old woman, disenfranchised by the deaths of her husband and sons, is followed doggedly by the loyal daughter-in-law. And Ruth's words, "Whither thou goest I will go," have echoed through centuries of wedding songs.

This was no wedding scene however. Quite the contrary. The wedding celebrations seemed over for these women. And so were the funerals. This passage, so spuriously used nowadays, was a pact between two desperate women. The rest of the story, of course, concerns the scheming of the two women, directed by the mother-in-law, to catch another kinsman, the rich farmer Boaz, as husband for the widowed Ruth and a protector for Naomi in her old age. This is one of the few tales from the Old Testament where there was no miraculous intervention to set things straight, no angel visitors, no dreams to be interpreted, no bushes burning or seas parting. Nature simply took its course, aided by the crafty Naomi. And in the end we see her, content at last, dandling Obed, the future grandfather of David, on her knee.

Last of all there is David himself. Like Joseph, he was the baby of the family, and his own brothers did not have much use for him until he became king. But he and Jonathan, the king's son and heir, adopted one another as brothers and established a relationship that was to prove the closest kinship either ever knew. It cut through all the political intrigue that plagues royal households. For this foster brother Jonathan set aside all his ambitions as heir to Saul's throne. And David in later years, long after Jonathan's death, remained true to his promise to protect Jonathan's son Mephibosheth.

There we have just about all the examples of family devotion to be found in the Old Testament. Not much of a harvest: two dutiful sons, a deferential uncle, a little girl baby-sitting her brother, a mother dedicating and relinquishing her long-awaited son, a mother-in-law story, and two foster brothers refusing to fight one another.

Notice how none of these stories involve what we would consider a united domestic situation or a complete family unit. The scrupulous behavior of Shem and Japheth toward their father is exactly what divides the sons of Noah. Land splits up Lot and Abraham. Baby Moses fished out of the bulrushes by Pharaoh's daughter results in a family divided and separated, this time by political circumstances. And how many modern mothers would find it wholesome maternal behavior to hand over their toddlers, as Hannah did, to the tutelage of an old priest who hadn't been too successful raising his own sons?

The two remaining examples are not even built on blood relationships. Ruth, the determined daughter-in-law, was in fact a foreigner, completely outside the bounds of custom that would have obligated an Israelite. And Naomi had no plump, comforting bosom on which to console her. She was a woman sunk deeply in depression, knowing full well what the life of a widow without protection in the world would bring. David and Jonathan, whose devotion to one another was as rare as it was touching, perhaps achieved such a state of fraternal peace precisely because they had not fought in the same nest as children. But their friendship could not extend to the foster father, Saul. He feared David and despised his own son as a weakling unwilling to rid himself of this threat to his own throne.

Not a single, intact family group among them. Only bits and pieces of families, broken off from the whole, patched together as best they could manage. The disintegration of the family is a byword today, a catch phrase by which we can reduce our private anguish to a pitch that can be borne in public. But this dissolution is not modern. It did not begin yesterday. The family, that abstract entity upon which we stake our psychological fortunes, began its break-up with the murder of Abel. The fact that it has held together at all, in the ancient past or under current stress, is only a matter of grace, like life itself.

Jonathan and David's kinship goes against all reasonable expectations. Ruth sticking with Naomi, when she had no institutional imperative to do so and though the old lady could have only been a liability, surprises us. And why should Shem and Japheth have passed up a chance to show up their father for the foolish drunkard he was? All these examples are odd, inexplicable, broken bits of shattered families. They provide a generous supply of material for the imaginative operation of grace.

Joseph, in fact, told quite plainly how human families, battered by the bad faith of their members, nevertheless are saved from self-destruction, snagged with the hook of creative compassion. His brothers were fearful that, after the death of their father Jacob, Joseph would take his revenge on them. But he reassured them. "You intended to harm me, but God intended it for good to accomplish what is now being done, the saving of many lives."

The human family has always been God's great salvage operation. How could God have intended betrayal, premeditated murder, or slavery for good? It boggles our minds. Fortunately God's imagination is more fecund than our own.

This sparse harvest of edifying domesticity may surprise us

when we consider how frequently the Bible is pointed to as the textbook for establishing and maintaining a happy family. Supposedly all we need do is follow certain biblical injunctions—and we will be guaranteed a healthy, happy, wise household. Certainly some instructions exist in the Bible, along with *Honor thy father and mother* and *Provoke not thy children to wrath*. But better men and women than we have failed at the task of following them, or, following them, have seen their children come to a bad end anyway.

What is the remedy for the sibling rivalry that tears families apart, the internecine jealousies that set one member against another like warring factions within a single kingdom. "Behold, how good and pleasant it is when brothers dwell in unity!" Indeed. But that is merely a description of the truth, not a formula for finding it. No doubt both Jacob and David admonished their quarrelsome children with that or similar platitudes. But did it insure their illumination and reform? No more than the Lord's own admonition to Cain. Back comes the petulant response, "Am I my brother's keeper?" Even in an age as unfamiliar with biblical quotations as our own, we continue to hurl it in the faces of both our earthly parents and our heavenly Father.

There was never a need for Freud to go as far afield as Greek mythology to find the type of a rebellious son, intent on usurping the place of the father. There were plenty of examples from the literature of his own heritage, starting with Adam and running through Absalom. There are, in fact, many more unhappy family histories recounted there than happy ones. Murder, sexual violation, abuse, adultery, jealousy, greed.

It is tempting to ferret out the rules found in the biblical manuals like Proverbs and to hand them out like prescriptions for foolproof parenting. But it is also misleading. The other part of the Scriptures, the stories, show no great success in applying the rules with any regularity. From that first birth, the human family has been one long saga of travail and sorrow. If it only took applying rules to get results, there would have been no need for that other birth, centuries later, of the Child whose obedience to his Father and perfect fellowship with his brothers and sisters are both judgment and salvation for us all.

CHAPTER ELEVEN

Faith and Our Father

As a child I used to wonder what would have become of me if I had been born into a family of New Guinea cannibals instead of Texas Southern Baptists. During the 1950s children were frequently admonished to thank God that they had been born in America, as though they had been the lucky winners in some prenatal sweepstakes. Thus there was early implanted in my mind a certain sense of having narrowly and inexplicably escaped not only poverty, ignorance, and totalitarian regimes, but perdition itself.

What if I had been born in Afghanistan and my parents had been Muslims instead of Christians? Logically, I knew I would in all likelihood have grown up believing as they did. It was not reasonable to expect that I would have been the object of a special revelation in order to save me from their errors. And it certainly never occurred to me that I might have gone through the same sort of apostasy as a cannibal that I did as a Christian. It is in fact with such hypothetical situations that I used to undermine my inherited faith. Religion, I learned, was merely a psychosocial phenomenon, another of the culturally conditioned accouterments one inherited, along with the English language and indoor plumbing, from one's parents.

There was no denying that I *had* inherited my religion. When you begin to be taken to church at the tender and helpless age of six weeks, how are you to protect yourself from the insidious influences you are so unwittingly exposed to there? And since I lived in an age where cultural conditioning—what used to be called without apology "tradition"—is tacitly despised, something to be grown out of, I began to distrust my faith for the very reason that I had been taught it.

Now I didn't stop eating with forks and knives and take up chopsticks just because such cutlery was the condition of the culture I had inherited. Nor did I go about in a loincloth, even though that would have made more sense during most of Texas's muggy months. But the fact that I had inherited my faith seemed somehow to cheapen its value for me. How could what was really the True Faith have been entrusted to such a clannish, provincial, rickety way of preserving it? Essential biological information was coded precisely and elegantly in those long, twining molecules coiled in each nucleus of my cells. Why, then, was the knowledge of God shuttled about in such a precarious, cavalier fashion? In order to be fair, shouldn't all people be supplied with identical information? As my mother never tired of reminding me, not everyone had had my advantages. She said it intending to elicit better behavior from me, but it only convinced me that if I were possessed of advantages withheld from others, then God was unfair and his claim on us less than binding.

Perhaps if I had been possessed of a more genuinely scientific bent at the time, my expectations would not have been so unrealistic, for certainly not everyone has the same information coded in their genes. My very physical being, from the shape of my nose to my natural immunity to mumps, was a matter of inheritance. I could just as reasonably have complained that I was born a human instead of a frog. It is simply the shape of human life to be limited to one existence, one set of circumstances at a time. Only in the recent mechanistic age has the illusion been fostered that we can and ought to transcend these limiting conditions.

For some reason, religion has been particularly singled out to bear the onus of cultural conditioning. Of all possible examples of cultural diversity, it was judged to be a sham simply because it was transmitted through tradition. Yet no one felt his language was invalid because he had learned to speak it at his mother's knee, or found his genes to be lacking in reality since he had had no say in selecting them.

It is only lately that I have thought about turning the question upside-down. If we find ourselves saddled with a load of inherited baggage, whether genetic or cultural, a load we had no part in choosing, what about the situation from our parents' point of view? Did they have any greater say in what they got as offspring? Were they able to shop for their child? And if they had been given that option, would they have chosen *us*? Weren't they taking a chance, buying the big surprise box at the rummage sale?

No doubt every expectant mother incubates in her mind the idea of what her child will be like, just as she gestates in her body the exploding blob of tissue. It seems impossible not to form images of this creature one hopes to shape to perfection. Saint Chrysostom even suggested that we give our children great, ringing biblical names in order that they might have a standard to live up to in times of doubt and conflict. Still, whether it lives up to those expectations, whether the dream is fulfilled or not, the child remains nevertheless the parents' inheritance. The code they have bequeathed to the child identifies it irrevocably as their own.

I may have thought a good deal, and not always gratefully, about the Christian faith as my inheritance, but only recently have I considered that situation the other way around. That is to say, are we not ourselves God's inheritance, the burden he is saddled with?

Israel is, in fact, called "the inheritance of Yahweh." Moses, on the threshold of the Promised Land, had the audacity to point out to the Lord how he would be disgraced in the eyes of the heathen if he abandoned his people.

> *O Sovereign Lord, do not destroy your people, your own inheritance that you redeemed by your great power and brought out of Egypt with a mighty hand. Remember your servants Abraham, Isaac and Jacob. Overlook the stubbornness of this people, their wickedness and their sin. Otherwise, the country from which you brought us will say, "Because the Lord was not able to take them into the land he had promised them, and because he hated them, he brought them out to put them to death in the desert." But they are your people, your inheritance that you brought out by your great power and your outstretched arm.*

We don't much talk in terms of our being God's inheritance any more, but it was a notion that had a good deal of currency in the ancient world. All deities had as their "inheritance" the people who lived in the land the god laid claim to. Today when we speak of the Canaanite gods, we mean the deities that belonged to the people inhabiting Canaan. To our modern minds it was the people who possessed the gods. But the Canaanites themselves would have understood the term to mean the gods that were attached to that particular bit of geography, the gods that owned that country—and of course the people who lived there were thrown in with the bargain. The gods "inherited" them. So long as conditions were such that the land was habitable, the gods would retain their portion of worshipers. But if the gods failed to supply the necessary crops and rainfall, or if they allowed famine or pestilence to rack the land, then they would lose their following, either because the people would be forced to migrate to another deity's turf or because they would die off. A god needed his "inheritance," his people, in order to maintain his position as a deity. A god with no worshipers was out of a job.

The notion that gods were attached to a particular place is illustrated in the story of Naaman, the Syrian general who became infected with leprosy. After he had been healed by Elisha, the representative of Israel's God, he asked the prophet for two mule loads of Israelite earth to carry back with him to Syria so that he might be able to worship the Lord in his home country. And Elisha granted his request.

The people of Israel were Yahweh's inheritance. They had made a wobbly sort of pact with him in the desert when they hadn't much choice but to follow the wandering pillar of cloud and fire. The patriarchal history emphasized how a single family line became the channel for the divine promises passed from Abraham to Isaac to Jacob. The national history broadens that channel to include the entire people of Israel when they became Yahweh's inheritance in the desert. "Save your people and bless your inheritance," implores the psalmist. "Be their shepherd and carry them forever."

Later, this concept of the Lord "inheriting" his people achieved a new dimension. When David became king, the Lord made this promise to him: "I will be his father, and he will be my son." This promise was retained, even after the downfall of the nation of Israel and Judah, as a guarantee of the future Messiah.

Now the Canaanites and indeed all the people of the Middle East shared some notion of the fatherhood of at least one of their gods. Homer called the primary Greek deity Father Zeus. And Plato, in a more philosophical vein, referred to the "Maker and Father of the universe." The creative power of the deity is what most pagans meant when they named such a being Father —either a dimly apprehended life force that supplied the essence of fecundity to the world, or the more intellectualized prime mover. Even today many aboriginal cultures support mythologies that tell of a divine being from whom their tribe is physically descended. It seems to be an apprehension that saturates human history. That element is not entirely missing even in the Christian Scriptures where the genealogy of Jesus is traced by Luke to "Adam, son of God."

Calling God "Father" can have different levels of meaning certainly. Jesus' Jewish adversaries often laid claim to their special status as children of Abraham, but they also, in John's gospel, asserted that "The only Father we have is God himself." How then could they bring charges against Jesus on the grounds that he claimed to be the Son of God? Quite obviously they sensed that he meant something different by the name than they did. For him it was no mere pious sentiment, no thin moralistic identification.

Jesus did not use that name in order to acknowledge the philosophical abstraction of God as the Creator of the universe, nor did he have in mind some link to a distant ancestor of his race. He did not call God his Father in order to underscore the special calling his people had from God nor to emphasize the moral likeness they bore to this demanding deity. There may have been some nugget of truth in all these partial understandings, but none of them went far enough. Not even the messianic promise to David. That promise may have hinted at a potential paternity, but even it could not encompass the fullness of that Fatherhood.

The Only Begotten Son. Begotten not made. Of one substance with the Father. No wonder the Jewish adversaries were horrified. This must have sounded like the old paganism to them, shorn of even the respectable Hellenic abstractions such primitive and dangerous ideas had been reduced to by the time of that creed.

And the phrases still sound strange and even ominous to our ears today. When we say them, we have the feeling we are assenting to more than we know. We are comparatively comfortable with one generation praising the works of God to another, with that remembrance being handed down like a genetic code raised to consciousness. We may come to see the value of this kind of spiritual inheritance, even with its unavoidably transient cultural trappings. And we definitely find those ties that bind God to us as *his* inheritance a consolation. But how are we to understand this historical human being, this flesh and blood with dirty feet and a parched throat, walking around Palestine, talking about his Father in very particular, unphilosophical terms?

His *Abba.* All human languages have simple, baby-talk syllables for the familiar forms of parental names. Daddy, Mamma. Papa, *Abba.* A term the Jews of his day seldom, if ever, used for God. It frightens us, as it did them, to think of being so familiar with God.

But except on the cross where the despairing cry from Psalm 22 rang out, Jesus never called upon God with any other name on earth but Father. Even when speaking *about* him, he most often used this name. He taught about the kingdom in parables, but the ruler of that kingdom is always *Father*. He encouraged his followers to use this name, telling them that their heavenly Father knew their needs, gave them good gifts, was determined even to give them the kingdom. While acknowledging his own unique position as the Son, Jesus was eager to have others claim this same Father.

He told parables of fathers and their children. It is in fact through these stories that we get some idea of the untenable position God has put himself in with regard to us. There is no other way we could have learned to pity God except through these paradigms of paternity.

Look, for example, at the two sons Jesus described in Matthew. The first one flatly refuses to go work in the vineyard. The second son promises to go but does not. Even given the fact that the first son changes his mind and goes to work after all, the father doesn't seem to have been fortunate in his offspring. One treated him with disrespect and the other lied to him. The father had to be satisfied with whatever scrap of obedience, however reluctant, he could get from those boys.

Or examine the better-known story of the Prodigal Son. Here is a child who exploits his father's good nature, not only by demanding his share of the inheritance prematurely, but by scheming, even as he sits starving among the pigs, how to finagle his way back into his father's good graces. Nor is the father more blessed in his elder son. This one may have lacked the more flagrant vices of his younger brother, but neither had he inherited the generous nature of his father. He even lacked the capacity to enjoy the privileges of the household and instead relished his own spite and vengefulness toward his brother.

Who would *choose* to be the father of such children? His attempts to provide for his children, to give them good gifts, are thwarted by their own pride and impatience. His efforts to enlist their help meet with only marginal success. No wonder the first thing Jesus had to teach his disciples when they learned to call upon his Father was to hallow his name. It strikes us as a somewhat bewildering formality, that phrase: *Our Father ... hallowed be thy name*. But considering our similitude to these sons of the parables, these children who, one way and another, dishonor their father's name, it is a phrase we need to use often as a means of reaffirming our lapsed intentions of reverence.

Because we have been parents, we know some measure of the pain of God. From a child's point of view, disobedience is merely one of the options open to him when presented with the demands of his parents. Any pain associated with disobedience is purely a matter of getting caught and punished. But the pain to the parent is much more radical and reaches to the root of the child's being. The parent knows that disobedience, deceit, and contempt are not merely temporary activities to be chosen or not chosen as fancy takes the child. The parent knows that these are the seeds of self-destruction and that once they have taken root, they will bring down to death that shining thing the child might have been. That is the true pain of disobedience, and it is the parent who bears it.

Those who would use the Scriptures, or at any rate the parables, as a paradigm for child-rearing had better beware. The father of the parables is a most permissive parent. He does not coerce obedience. he does not refuse requests on the grounds that he knows what is best for the child. There is absolute freedom to come and go, to do or not do, just as the child wills. And always in the background lurks the disaster that freedom often brings.

But what of that child who *is* obedient, the one who is a child of this Father in a way that marks him off from the rest of us? The world's one child who did consent to be born? Is his fate any happier? Is there a fairy-tale ending to his story?

What of the heir in the parable who came to collect his father's share of the vineyard's fruits from the tenants who had rented it? Supposedly he knew how his predecessors had been treated, how they were insulted and beaten and turned out of the place. Yet he went anyway. And the reward for his obedience was death.

The father's fierce indignation against the outrage done his son is terrible to contemplate. He tolerated the humiliations to himself in the persons of his emissaries, but the desecration of his son he does not abide.

Consider what a tour de force, what a literary device of dazzling virtuosity this parable is. It consists of a story within a story. Think of the dramatic irony of the situation. For here stands the very Son of the parable, knowing he is going to be murdered and thrown out of the vineyard, telling the story to the tenants themselves while the inevitable climax still looms ahead of them and the Father watches on in agony.

The Father must judge, must right the wrongs that have been done in his vineyard. Otherwise he is none of the other names that we call him: Almighty, Creator, Savior, Victor. But it is because he is *Father* that he himself suffers, and suffers most, from his own judgment. "Cast away from you that doctrine of devils," stormed George MacDonald, "that Jesus died to save us from our Father. There is no safety, no good of any kind but with the Father, His Father and our Father."

Charles Péguy, the French convert and poet, stuns us with his picture of just how vulnerable the Father is to our claims, how irresistible our entreaties are when preceded by that fatal patronym:

> (God speaks)
> *"Our Father who art in heaven . . .*
> He knew very well what he was doing that day, my Son
>   who loved them so,
> When he placed that barrier between them and me,
>   *Our Father*
> *Who art in heaven,* those three or four words,
> That barrier which my anger and perhaps my justice
>   will never cross.
> Those three or four words which go ahead like a beautiful pointed prow in front of a miserable ship,
> And which cut through the waves of my wrath
> And when the point of the prow has passed, the ship
>   passes, and the whole fleet after it.
>
> . . . .
>
> And the ship is my own Son, laden with all the sins of
>   the world,
> And the point of the ship: those are my Son's two hands
>   joined together.
> And that point: those are the three or four words,
>   *Our Father . . .*
>
> . . . .

Like a great fleet of the ancients, like a fleet of triremes
Advancing to attack the King.
And I—what would you have me do? I am being at-
    tacked,
And in this fleet, in this innumerable fleet,
Every *Our Father* is like a mighty warship
Which has its own pointed prow, *Our Father* . . .
Turned toward me, and which advances behind its
    pointed prow."

Because we have been parents ourselves we can understand how
God is vulnerable to the cries of his children, even in their sins.

Is there any other way we *could* have understood a God
who suffers except by means of this eternal Father and Son who
make of every mortal relationship merely a metaphor?

We ransack the Scriptures in desperation, looking for the
magic formula that will protect us and our families from disasters
that lurk in every decision we make and every circumstance we
don't make. We want protection both from our own wills and our
own inadequacies. We look to the doctrines of the church with the
same calculating eye. Surely the Trinity is meant to teach us
something, some great secret of human life. Surely it is a figure of
speech devised for our edification, a useful technique for teaching
family values.

Our motives are not entirely ignoble. We want to be good
stewards of these beings entrusted to our care for a space. It is not
wrong to long to hear, "Well done, thou good and faithful servant."

But there must come some point when we realize that this
parental part we play is not in itself ultimate. Yet those who are
most conscientious in performing their parental duties are sometimes most blinded by their own swollen, if good, intentions.

God the Father does not exist in order to provide us with a
proper pattern for parenting. It is he who has made us for himself,
not we who make him for our handy illustration of perfection. We
are the shadows his significance casts, the created refractions of his
uncreated light. The whole burning truth that is the Trinity would
incinerate even the best of our poor imitations if we were capable
of getting close enough to take its measurement. We need to get

over the notion of using God as a convenience, even for the highest mortal motives.

We have families; they are a reflection, however feeble, of the nature of the Spirit that created them, of the participating life of Love and Beloved. Let us not fall into an easy and deceptive reversal of that truth, that the Trinity is a reflection of the perfect Christian family.

All families, both heavenly and earthly, are named from the one true Father, Paul tells us. Father is a divine name only lent to creatures. God the Father thought up families for us in order to teach us something of who *he* is. Even the first tenuous form of reciprocal identity exchange among the single-celled *Ciliata* gives us a glimmer of Christ's claim that he was in the Father and the Father in him. And the mother who waited at the foot of the cross, who had been told at her son's birth that a sword would pierce her own soul also, is a visible sign of the Father's suffering which we cannot see.

Call no man your father on earth, commanded Jesus, *for you have one Father, who is in heaven.* All the rest are mere copies of the real thing. "She's just like her father," we often say of our older daughter. She has the same thick, dark hair, the same long bones, the same quick, mercurial temperament. But beyond that there is one whose image she truly bears, a Father whose life is more deeply rooted in her than those dominant genes, than even the life that seems to be her own. And so it is for us all. We must be, eventually, just like our Father, or not be at all. We must grow up into the full stature of Christ, himself just like his Father, or be the self-aborted fetuses of futility. That is our destiny, our destination. We either move toward it or into nothingness.

Call no man your father on earth. With that one imperative Jesus freed parents from a burden we are not capable of carrying, from the shame we feel at our inevitable failures. It may strike some ears as harsh, that injunction, on a level with the question, "Who are my mother and brothers and sisters?" Again, let those who look at the Bible as a scriptural Dr. Spock beware. Jesus was no circuit-speaker leading seminars on happy problems for happy families. His case histories of families are all tragedies. Even the ending to the parable of the prodigal is inconclusive. He

makes no promises of well-regulated domestic life for his followers. On the contrary, he assures them that his very presence will set
family members against one another.

I know the straws we grasp at to insure our children's
destiny. The classes, the workshops, the books all bent on figuring
out the proper dovetailing of parental guidance with youthful
independence. The delicate balancing of permissiveness and au-
thority. Mothers take their babies to the pediatrician to have their
feet tickled and their grasp measured, just as mothers used to take
them to the temple to be blessed. Special car seats are designed to
protect infants from a headon collision. There are organizations to
cultivate breast-feeding, arrange child-sized sports, oversee education, prevent drug abuse. Has there ever been a civilization in the
history of the world so scrupulous about nurturing its children, so
intent on finding the magic formula for effective parenting? Has
there ever been a nation so obsessed by guilt at its failure?

And yet good, conscientious parents sometimes produce a
presidential assassin, while an alcoholic, unemployed shoe salesman produces the president the assassin tries to shoot.

I am never so aware of grace as when I look at my
daughters. I see it shining all around them like a nimbus. How did
they ever manage to grow up with straight legs and teeth, good
grades and a moral sense surpassing my own at their age, except by
the grace of God? In their childhood years neither the proper kind
of car seats nor play groups had been invented yet. Nor on the
other hand did they have the alternative advantages of my now
archaic upbringing—the sturdy Sunday schooling where the Bible
stories soaked into one's bloodstream. From time to time I am
shocked at the holes I stumble across in their stock of spiritual
information. How can a Presbyterian minister's daughter not
know what Pentecost is?

I shudder to think of the influences they were exposed to in
their tender, impressionable years when we were growing up together. Their upbringing has been haphazard at best, and there
have been desperate and dangerous failures on both their parents'
parts.

Yet there they are. Alive. Healthy. Intelligent. To my mind
beautiful. *This is the Lord's doing: it is marvelous in our eyes.*

And what of their destiny, the question of that high calling with which I began this book? What do I do to undergird, direct, sustain, set on its legs a wobbly little dream like destiny? Especially when, however beautiful they appear to me now, I know their final destiny is to be transformed into the likeness of their true Father, changed from glory into glory? How does a mortal mother cultivate immortal glory for a child who is not really hers but God's?

I hardly dare breathe upon the bloom of that vision for fear of blighting it. I have to confess, as Joseph did to his brothers, "Am I in the place of God?"

I am only a chrysalis case that wrapped them round till time came for them to break out into the light on their own. They cling to the twig now, nascent and trembling, drying their slowly lifting wings in the sun. I watch, transfixed. The only breath I dare to take is prayer.

Like all created things, the family is conditional. It exists provisionally, on God's good pleasure. It is not in itself ultimate. We should beware of building a religion on it or even around it. But insofar as God himself has allowed us to call him Father, and indeed makes us his children, the family is a reflection raised nearer to its source of reality than perhaps any other image presented to our understanding. I am convinced that the family is one of those ways God maintains a witness to himself in the world. When I look at the tracks I have left across time, I see that the path provided for me was kept, one way and another, by my family. If I had any sense of my value, any idea of destiny, it developed from that rich food on which I was fed.

At the same time, it has all been a matter of grace, a gift. Again, when I look at my own situation and those of other families, I see that at any moment things could have gone differently. I could have continued rejecting my family's faith. Many do. Many intelligent, thoughtful people have. The children of believers are given no special guarantees.

For all of us there is a moment when the world cracks, when the principalities and powers that rule all things temporal are forced back and grace flashes across our vision, illuminating the salvation that surrounds us like the sea. Then all mortal flesh must keep silence while the eternal Father waits.

Epilogue

The bustle in a house
The morning after death
Is solemnest of industries
Enacted upon earth—
The sweeping up the heart,
And putting love away
We shall not want to use again
Until eternity.
                    —Emily Dickinson

There is one fact that cannot be omitted from an account of families. It is that hardest and coldest fact presented to the human understanding; it is the one inevitable experience shared by all families. Some of the people with whom I began this record have already died by the time I am finishing it. Time, like an ever-rolling stream, has borne us away from one another.

My grandmother died in her sleep of a heart attack just before sunup on Valentine's Day. My grandfather woke suddenly to find her lying still and stiff beside him. She had had what appeared to be indigestion earlier in the evening, and he had sat up with her until she began to feel easier.

She had just turned eighty the month before. Because the death occurred at their farm home twenty miles out of town, an inquest was necessary to satisfy the law. The justice of the peace arrived to find her body stretched out on the bed in her nightgown, her ankles neatly crossed in her customary sleeping position, and a white shell-patterned sweater pinned across her chest. My grandfather had refused to cover her face with the sheet, and except for her profound imperturbability in the midst of the surrounding commotion, one would have thought her asleep. There was no need to close her eyelids. Only her heavy mouth sagged a bit.

It was hard to believe she was gone, fled from the stolid, thick body that had served her tolerably well for fourscore years. It had borne six children, had never been violated by a surgeon's knife, and had worked with the dogged dependability of a draft horse. Now it lay there, patiently waiting for the undertaker.

Meanwhile, one had the impression that Granny, hiking her aluminum walker along before her like a skeletal pulpit, had hightailed it off across the back pasture where the morning mist was just rising and had disappeared into the trees.

Escaped. Escaped once and for all from getting up and fixing my grandfather's breakfast biscuits. Escaped from all the jars and boxes she had cleaned out and saved over the years and that sat, empty, stacked in cupboards and closets. Escaped from all the birthday and Mother's Day cards accumulated over nearly half a century. Escaped from an imminent Golden Wedding Anniversary. Escaped from thirty grandchildren and their thirty more great-grandchildren.

I was the oldest of all these. Technically, she was my stepgrandmother, though as she was married to my grandfather years before I was ever born, she was the only grandmother I had. It was, in fact, my mother who got the telephone call and sped the twenty miles on the blacktopped farm road to arrive at the latched front screen and hear her father sobbing inside, unable to make him hear her pounding on the door. Finally a neighbor lady heard her and shuffled out onto the porch in housecoat and slippers to let her in.

Father and daughter sit for hours waiting for the justice of the peace and the ambulance. Meanwhile, other relatives begin to arrive. My grandfather's cousin, Silas Quincy, sits in front of the space heater with him and keeps up conversation by saying, "Remember when we used to . . . ?" The memories disinterred in front of the fire are mostly of their youth, before either of them were married. They seem to comfort my grandfather.

My mother makes coffee, and after that, breakfast. She fries sausage and eggs and makes biscuits as close to Granny's recipe as she can. They all eat heartily.

By mid-morning other of the children begin to arrive: the youngest daughter, who has perhaps been closest to Granny, and her husband. My grandfather and the youngest daughter sit together on the front porch, heaving the air in and out of their lungs in that extravagance of inhalation mysterious and essential to human grief. After a while my mother comes out onto the porch and takes my grandfather by the arm. "All right, daddy. Let's go inside now." He leaves off crying, goes back inside, and takes up his place before the fire again.

The two sisters go into the bedroom and search through the dresser drawers and in the closet for clothes to take to the funeral home. The task is peculiarly like preparing to dress a doll. The clothes will have no actual functional value. They are chosen—the underwear, the dress, the ornaments—for purely symbolic reasons. They first choose a loose red dress that was one of Granny's favorites, but afterward decide against it and choose instead a pale green two-piece suit that is at once dressier and, as they describe it, "softer."

At the funeral home, an institution that has already processed the bodies of two of his children in years past, my grandfather picks out a casket costing $1250. A son-in-law who is a minister is with him and advises against a costlier one, pointing out the biological inevitabilities that assault the flesh. They settle on a pine box in which to seal the casket and then go home again to wait till the body is ready—about four-thirty, the mortician promises.

At home, more people. The family is large, and cousins, of whatever degree removed, feel their ties of significant strength to make themselves a part of the mourning tableau. Details of feeding this multitude and lodging those coming from a distance occupy my mother. Also there is the alcoholic daughter to be located and, once found, provided with a sober driver.

So there they all are assembled at the appointed hour in the afternoon at the funeral home. Another daughter and a son, both with their families, are yet to arrive but are not expected till late in the night. The rest enter the parlor, subdued by silent carpeting, where my grandmother now lies on a satin cushion. She never had a house with carpets in her life and certainly never slept on satin sheets. But death allows certain liberties. Her topknot, gray and sparse, is tidily in place as she wore it living. Everyone agrees she looks nice, very natural—except for one detail noticed by the alcoholic daughter who insists the fingernail polish come off. If anything would set my grandmother spinning in her grave, nail polish would do it.

When everyone is satisfied with the undertaker's work, they leave again, except for my grandfather and another son-in-law, the well-to-do one who stays behind with him to settle financial arrangements. After the others have cleared out, my grandfather walks up to the casket and stands there a while, looking down. He nods his head as though satisfied with the results, turns, and takes a few steps toward the door. Then he turns again and comes back to look once more. He purses his mouth, nods again, and then walks over the muffled floor of the viewing room and into the hall where the well-to-do son-in-law is waiting.

"I want to see the head man of this place," he says.

Together they find the office and the manager, who invites them to be seated in the enveloping Naugahyde chairs. My grandfather prefers to stand, however.

"How much do I owe you?" he asks.

The mortician makes a gesture as though to wave away the intrusive aroma of money and says they can send a bill later. But my grandfather insists on settling the account at once. With evident discomfort, the man punches out the numbers on his calculator. They total $2678. My grandfather draws a bundle of bills from his pocket, peels them off with his crooked old man's fingers, counting carefully but steadily, and hands him the entire amount in cash.

"Now we're square," he says as he picks up the receipt and

walks out, followed by the well-to-do, bewildered son-in-law.

They have settled on the next afternoon for the funeral. This is unusual in the family. It is almost always three, at times four or even five days, before the body actually makes it to its resting place. But as all the children will be there by the next day, there seems to be no point in waiting.

That night, two daughters, the youngest and the alcoholic, sit in the hushed parlor with the body. This, too, used to be customary. My grandfather himself sat up with the bodies of his dead son and daughter in this same room. But this time, when he's told that these two daughters are keeping watch at the casket, he asks, "What for?"

Four days after the funeral I go back to the cemetery with my mother just at sunset. At the west entrance lie the bones of Sam Houston, the early hero of Texas. He is marked with a monument of historical import now, but for many years his grave was virtually abandoned. In the extreme northeast corner of the cemetery, jostling the wrought-iron arrow-tipped fence, is my grandmother. At her head lies a stepdaughter, my mother's sister, who fell over dead in Granny's kitchen several years ago, quite without warning. Beyond her is one of Granny's own sons, a member of the Army Medical Corps. He went over a cliff near Heidelberg in an ambulance in 1956. Three more bodies, those of my grandfather's mother, one of his brothers, and an infant nephew, make up the rest of the little congregation under the cedar trees. My mother points out that there is room for only four more in the plot.

The flowers from the funeral have been propped up against the iron railing by the workmen who have had more practical matters on their minds. My mother sets about plucking out the blooms that have held up the best in the chill, damp February air. Red, white, and pink carnations. Some deathly lavender dahlias, several spikes of pussy willows, and even three or four red roses. She straightens out the bedraggled satin ribbons with glue-and-glitter writing on them that hang from the spindly metal easels: "Brothers and sisters," it says in silver sparkles on one. "Goree Prison Unit" on another. Then she begins unpinning the florist's tags from each wreath.

I've already been sent to the funeral office to get extra boxes of acknowledgment cards to mail to these flower folk. The cards have an embossed rose on the left side and declare in elaborate script that

The family of

acknowledge with grateful
appreciation the kind expression
of your sympathy.

My mother has already filled in the blank space with my grand-mother's name on several boxes of these.

Someone has been there before us and has taken a few daffodils and irises out of another arrangement and has stuck them upright in the dirt at the head of the mound of red clay humped up like a potato cellar. My mother takes a large cruciform of palmate leaves studded with faded flowers and twitches it up over the mound like a quilt. "There," she says.

One of the fresher bouquets she sets on her sister's headstone. Then she takes one of the green metal easels to which is attached plastic orange chrysanthemums and a plaid ribbon and plants it firmly at Granny's distant feet. My mother is a tough-minded woman, and she stomps on the easel's bottom brace as though she were bruising the serpent's head until she has the whole affair firmly embedded in the red clay.

She has come to the cemetery not out of the thrifty desire to retrieve the still usable flowers, but to harvest the cards and to check for a silk flower bouquet that was to have been sent from the office where she works and which has either disappeared or never arrived. It seems a delicate point: should the missing silk flowers get an embossed rose acknowledgment card or not?

By now it is dusk, and the pickup truck waits outside the iron railing, full of Pyrex bowls and Tupperware containers, their owners' names blurred across adhesive tape labels, waiting to be delivered to the church. But still my mother lingers, straightening the ribbons again or jerking yet another upright carnation from among its heavy-headed fellows.

The haze that hangs, palpable, over us and Sam Houston

there away to the west is pink, going off to lavender. The naked
oak tree tracery is blackening against the sky, and the air down in
the stone-filled dell is silvered with the mist that rises in the evening from the sandy loam. Across the road the moon glows gold,
large and low. It seems so full and heavy. How will it ever heave
itself up the sky, lightening to its proper papery silver?

My mother takes a final look around at her housekeeping.
There seems to be nothing left to do.

Nothing is so domestic as death. Every death is a death in
the family, somebody's family. Even violent death on a distant
battlefield reverberates along nerves as lengthily proportioned to
the world as those single cells stretched in our body between the
lowest vertebra and the farthest toe; reverberates until it reaches
home, where it reels back and forth between the walls of the house
and the heart. It is the family that does the final sweeping up of
that dust we are all made of. Transients, orphans, outcasts, those
who have outlived their kin, even these must be tucked away by
some surrogate family, some funeral home.

Some time later I go walking in the woods behind my
parents' house. There, down in a ravine, is their garbage dump.
Living out in the country, one has to dispose of one's own wasted
substance, a fact of life happily obscured from those who live in
towns. Paper has to be separated for burning and kitchen scraps
either fed to the dogs or buried. What is left are all the cans and
bottles, broken appliances, scraps of carpet, worn-out water heat-
ers. All this is taken down to the dumping ground and used to stop
the wash in the ravine.

One comes upon it in the woods and stops, startled, suddenly confronted with this embarrassing secret of human living.
It's like a wen on the world's fair face, and a human feels properly
shamefaced stumbling upon it. But there it is. Archaeological
layers dating back at least to 1940 when bleach bottles were made
of dark brown glass. There are a good many of them there. The
fluted blades of a push mower are gilded now with green rust.
Strips of discarded linoleum are laminated together like damp,
decaying leaves. Cans, the old kind, have rusted the color of the
pine needles that drift over them. Shapes made strange by obsoles-

cence, farm implements, chicken feeders, have sprouted a rough, furred coat of iron oxide.

All that is the bottom layer. Nearer the top are plastic jugs, bright yellow anti-freeze containers, red coffee can lids, pieces of white styrofoam picnic coolers. They sit there, season after season, impervious to rot and decay. The aluminum still shines.

The things we make can't die any more. The artifacts of human industry continue to haunt the earth, like ghosts that cannot be laid. We have invested all our immortality in our products. But, thank heaven, human beings are still biodegradable.

Inside my parents' house my grandfather sits now, reft of his wife and blinded by cataracts. He has thirty-seven days to wait for the doctor to try to inlay a new lens in his one good eyeball. He will not turn on the light but sits in the dark, figuring calculations in his head for a new house he wants to build and sometimes muttering the numbers of board feet or the price of tenpenny nails aloud. He does not want to die, but he will, even with a new eye and a new house.

The generations are moving up a notch. My mother sits at the kitchen counter filling out her retirement papers, deciding on beneficiaries, insurance plans. In a few years' turnings I will take my mother's place and she will be the matriarch. My own daughters will begin new families. Gradually the layers are laid upon layers, and finally, having been buried under new generations, will sink into the earth.

We use the phrase "womb-to-tomb" to describe the encroachment of the state's cold charity upon what used to be the family's province. Birth and death were both family matters. These days, we come in and go out at the hospital's door, although my grandmother craftily avoided that particular portal altogether. But even with hospitals, we are *born into* families. Shouldn't we go out by that same door?

Death is a fact just as essential to families as birth. We've lost the sense of that somehow. It is the tool meant to teach us our mortality. Mother Teresa has said that it is not dying that is so terrible, but dying alone, with no one to care. We come into life tied, quite literally, to another human being, moored to our mothers by a tough, slick rope of flesh. And when one of us leaves the womb of this world, the afterbirth of that passage into another life remains to be cleaned up. Hearts still have to be swept, memories sorted and stored, the refuse deposited on the dump. Decay is not indecent; neglect is. The slatternly accumulation of deaths unattended to and hearts littered with implacable, unregarded grief will, over the generations, suffocate our families and their faith like the layers of plastic and aluminum.

Two of those with whom I started this book have already been laid away in this east Texas soil. Perhaps that is why I have been so eager to write it. It is my means of sweeping up my heart.

We learn about death by becoming its intimate, by holding its hand at the end, closing its eyes on the last light. Very few among us have the courage for those domestic details of death these days. Yet only those who hold its hand can learn the mystery of mortality. And in the end, those who handle the mystery are the ones who keep the faith.

This book was composed and printed by
the Zondervan Kentwood Manufacturing Center.
Text and display type—Granjon—was set on
a Mergenthaler V-I-P phototypesetter.
Initial display letters are
FORMATT* No. 5107.
Binding was done by
Tapley/Rutter in Moonachie, New Jersey.